Believe in miracles!

Paul Tregas

THE MAKING OF A MIRACLE...
LEAGUE

THE MIRACLE LEAGUE OF GREEN BAY STORY

PAUL LIEGEOIS,
"THE MIRACLE MAN"

iUniverse, Inc.
New York   Bloomington

The Making of a Miracle...League
The Miracle League of Green Bay Story

Copyright © 2009 Paul Liegeois

iUniverse books may be ordered through booksellers or by contacting:

iUniverse
1663 Liberty Drive
Bloomington, IN 47403
www.iuniverse.com
1-800-Authors (1-800-288-4677)

ISBN: 978-1-4401-2451-8 (pbk)
ISBN: 978-1-4401-2482-2 (cloth)
ISBN: 978-1-4401-2452-5 (ebk)

Printed in the United States of America

iUniverse rev. date: 2/23/2009

To my many "friends" and to all persons
with Parkinson's disease.

Contents

PREFACE

The Miracle League of Green Bay is a 501c3, nonprofit, charitable organization, that provides an opportunity for children with physical and mental challenges, ages four to nineteen, to play baseball on a real team with real major league look-alike uniforms, in an organized league, regardless of their capabilities.

Its mission is:

- To provide opportunities for children with disabilities a chance to play Miracle League baseball, regardless of their capabilities.
- To promote community support and sponsorship of Miracle Leagues.
- To promote the construction of special facilities that meet the unique needs of Miracle League players and their families.

This book is my story, from inspiration to creation, of the Miracle League of Green Bay. At the time of our startup in 2006, we were among one hundred and seventy-five communities in the country having a Miracle League in this growing program. There are over two hundred communities participating today, as of this writing and still growing. Our rubber surface field was the seventy-fifth to be built. We have just completed our third season, two seasons of which were on our new field.

I receive many phone call inquiries from all over the country from newly interested community leaders looking at starting Miracle Leagues and have been asked about our experiences. I am flattered that anyone would call and am most happy to help, anytime. It is my hope that this book, a true account, would be helpful to any prospective Miracle League leader. I'm sure that your eventual story will be just as joyous and rewarding as mine. They all are.

I am thankful to my many, many friends and my family, Mary Jo, Nick, and Beau that have helped me in my mission. I am thankful also for the many, many *new* friends the Miracle League has given me the opportunity to make, for all of the Miracle League families that I have come to meet, their children, and for all of the volunteers it takes to make the Miracle League possible.

Paul Liegeois
Founder/Executive Director
Allouez Optimists Miracle League of Green Bay

FOREWORD

"The Miracle League is a wonderful project and one that Brett and I as well as The Brett Favre Fourward Foundation are very proud to have been a part of.

The dedication of people like Paul Liegeois and numerous other volunteers is what makes Green Bay, Wisconsin a truly special place and one we have been blessed to call home for so many years. God Bless!" ... **Deanna Favre**

"Over the last decade the (Brett Favre Fourward Foundation) has given out $4 million to dozens of charitable organizations, focusing its efforts on the kinds of kids who remind Favre of Ronnie Hebert. One recent beneficiary was the Miracle League of Green Bay, to which Favre donated $100,000 to help build a baseball facility with a specially wheelchair-friendly artificial surface. In addition to the field, Favre's money went toward a high-end public-address system and the retrofitting of the playground to make it more accessible to those with disabilities."

"These kids always had to sit and watch before," says Bruce Willems, whose 16-year-old daughter, Kyla, is a regular in the Miracle League. "Now they get to play, and you can't believe what it does for their self-esteem."

Sports Illustrated - *Brett Favre* - *Sportsman of the Year* Issue
December 10, 2007, by **Alan Shipnuck**

(Ronnie Hebert was a developmentally disabled man who served as an equipment manager on Brett Favre's youth baseball team and helped out with Brett's father's squads. Brett formed a lasting relationship with Ronnie ... **Alan Shipnuck –** *Sports Illustrated)*

I wish to especially thank the Favres for all that they have done to make the Miracle League a success. Brett and Deanna, we miss you!

Paul Liegeois

ACKNOWLEDGEMENTS

I would like to acknowledge and thank the following who have contributed to the production of this book:

Ginny Mason – Proof reading
Mary Jo Liegeois - Editing
Dianne Niemann – Final edit
Nick Liegeois – Graphic cover design and photo prep
Donn Bramer Photography – cover photos used for cover
    illustration
Michele Lemmens – Photography
Stu Goldman – For the inspiration to write a book
Kris Maz, Launch Film – for the author photo
Jeff Kralovetz, Ambrosius Studios - Photography
Dan Bollom and Lola (Bollom) Schroeder – book consultation

And, to the many, many other Miracle League children and their families that I could have written about.

PaulLiegeois

Life's Not Fair

It is Thursday morning, September 7, 2005. My wife, Mary Jo, and I are aboard a plane on our way to visit our good friends, Dean and Terre Alford in Atlanta, Georgia. Mary Jo is sitting in the window seat and I in the aisle seat where I can stretch my painful legs. It's Parkinson's disease. I've had it for several years now. First the miniscule signs, then the increasing tremor and rigidity. Swelling and restlessness in the legs is common, especially at night. Needless to say, I don't travel very well.

Oh, yes, I went through the denial phase and "Why me?" At this stage of my illness, when on medication, it would probably still not be noticable to an observer. But the reality has sunk in that this is something that isn't going to go away. I have just retired from my job of thirty-three years at Wisconsin Public Service. My health was a factor.

"What does the future hold for me?" I thought.

"I'm fifty-six years old and not ready to let Parkinson's disease rule my life."

Life's not fair, I thought.

I have been looking forward to this trip. It should do me some good.

Little did I know about fairness than from what life lessons I would come to experience.

THE INSPIRATION

As our flight takes us to Atlanta, Mary Jo and I can't help but reminisce along the way about the wonderful times we've had with the Alfords on occasions in the past. Dean and Terre are two of the finest and most hospitable people you could ever want to know. We don't see one another very often, but when we do, it's just like old times again, catching up on all that has gone on in one another's lives. There were the Olympics in Atlanta in 1996. The Alfords housed our family at their home for one of our most memorable vacations.

Then there was the speedboat cruise we, and our spouses, took on Dean's friend and co-worker, Chuck Thomas's Cigarette-type racer, off the coast of Florida, near Tampa. We all met there on a weekend after a business trip. On a beautiful sunny, hot, Sunday afternoon, which, coincidentally also was a date when the Green Bay Packers were in town and playing the Tampa Bay Buccaneers, we listened intently to the game on the radio. The boat traffic on that perfect afternoon seemed like a highway out on the Inter-coastal Waterway. Catching the wake of a large cruising yacht as it passed us in the opposite direction caught us all off guard and sent us airborne, grasping at one another's feet, just to stay onboard. We must have been going seventy miles per hour at the time and smacked that wake head-on. We survived to tell about it.

On another family trip we stopped in Georgia with our boys on our way through to visit my brother in Florida. Dean, who at the time, among other things, was a State Representative in the Georgia Legislature, took us along as guests in a mountain resort for a couple of nights where his Legislative Committee was on a retreat. Fishing was on the agenda. Something my sons will never forget.

As our house guests one time, we'd recall when Dean's steamy shower set off our fire alarm. Startled, and wondering if he should make a run for it, you should have seen the look on his face as he peeked out of the bathroom wondering what was going on.

As always, Dean knew how to entertain his clients whenever the opportunity arose. We were one of his clients. Often times he and Terre would be at the utility industry conferences we attended. Hosting a dinner or something, he always knew how to make the spouses happy. Our wives became friends too. I have known Dean Alford as a business associate and as a personal friend for over twenty years. Mary Jo and I looked forward to this visit as we did all the others. We would not be disappointed.

On many occasions over the past few years, the Alfords had invited us to come visit, come to a Georgia Tech football game some weekend, if we could. Dean, an avid Tech alumnus, has a skybox and had an open invitation for us to come for a game.

"Just check the game schedule" for a date when you and Mary Jo can come," he'd say. "Bring the boys, spend some time. I'll take time off."

Well, this year, having just retired in August (I hadn't told Dean about that yet) from my executive position at Wisconsin Public Service Corporation after thirty three wonderful years, I decided we would take him up on the offer and chose the Georgia Tech – North Carolina football game weekend to be their guests in their skybox. More on my retirement later.

"I wonder if I will recognize Dean?" Mary Jo said as we landed in Atlanta and I left her to watch for him while I got the bags. He was there to pick us up. And yes, unmistakably, Dean is the same, just a little more silver haired.

Not surprisingly, Dean had the day planned. We would go to the Alford's cottage on the lake, about a fifty mile ride, meet wife Terre and daughter Jacque there, have dinner at the marina nearby where Dean would also pick up his boat, and stay for the night. In the morning Dean would launch his ski boat (a simple task as it turns out, as his concrete driveway weaved right down into the water for boat launching) and take us all aboard for the ride while he pulled daughter, Jacque, on her wake board. We could tell that Jacque, sixteen years old at the time, was no rookie at this. She bobbed and weaved as dad cranked up the music aimed at the skier, and filled the ballasts of the specially equipped "wake" skiing boat, to make more wake. We met others that day out on the lake, friends of Jacque's, with parents in similarly equipped boats for wake boarding, who stopped and talked.

The afternoon we would head back to the city. Terre and Jacque would go one way, Dean would take Mary Jo and me with him in another direction. Dean had some business to do at the State Capital, and had to see the Dean of Engineering at Georgia Tech. Mary Jo and I accompanied him. Now the State Capitol building and Georgia Tech campus in Atlanta are relatively close to each other. At the Capitol, Dean stays involved as a member of the State Board of Education and serves as Chairman of the Governor's Education Finance Task Force. Here we would meet one of the State Representatives, the Chairperson of the Education Committee, as Dean stopped by the office to pick up a package.

On we went to the Georgia Tech campus and to the Dean's office. There we would be introduced to Don Giddens, Dean of the College of Engineering, as Dean Alford's "very good friends from Green Bay, Wisconsin."

"Green Bay?" Giddens said. " My daughter-in-law is from De Pere, Wisconsin." "Come into my office where I, in fact, have a picture of her."

In his office was a framed action poster of Olympic kayaker, Rebecca Bennett Giddens and another framed action poster of Don Giddens' son, also an Olympic kayaker. I do not know Rebecca personally, but do know that her interest in kayaking all was inspired by my late friend, Ray McLain, who taught kayaking lessons at the Green Bay YMCA, where Rebecca Bennett learned the sport, and who later went on to coach and train Rebecca for the Olympics. My employer, Wisconsin Public Service Corporation, in fact, also sponsored her training. Ray McClain attended the Olympics that year in Atlanta, 1996, where Rebecca won her medal. He worked as an official on the kayak slalom course. Ray was retired and established a guided tours kayaking adventure business in Central America before he died from cancer. I told Don this story...small world.

Dean led us on a tour of the athletic facilities of the Georgia Tech Stadium. First, it was a visit to the athletic training room, where we would meet up with Dean's son, Chandler Alford, an engineering student at Georgia Tech, and an Olympic Weightlifter, in the midst of his afternoon lifting session. We were thrilled to see him. He did not skip a beat in his repetitions as he conversed with us in his usual southern gentlemanly "yes, sir" and "yes, ma'am" demeanor.

That was back in 2005. Chandler has competed in Olympic Weightlifting for eight years. As of today, 2009, he has won four national titles, numerous city, state and regional titles, and has competed on the international platform, including Chile, Columbia, and Puerto Rico. Chandler is the current Collegiate National Champion, just competed in the USA Weightlifting Olympic Team Trials, and is now ranked seventeenth overall in the country. Now a senior, his next stop was to be the World University Games in Athens, Greece, during Thanksgiving 2008. That didn't take place, however, as his time for acedemics required to graduate was decidedly a priority.

Small in stature, but in the 77 kg (175 lb) weight class he snatches 125 kg (275 lbs) and clean and jerks 175 kg (385 lbs.). He just missed qualifying for the 2008 Olympics in Beijing. He plans to continue training for the 2012 Olympics. Needless to say, we are very proud for him.

We saw the athletic department as Dean took us through the inner perimeter of the Stadium, the coach's offices, including head football coach, Chan Gailey's office, the player's lounge, and the school's Hall of Fame. Dean was greeted by name everywhere we went. After a quick bite to eat at the famous Varsity Drive-In across the street from the campus, we headed for their home. We'd been at the Varsity before, a landmark-drive up and walk-up counter service order place. Fortunately we knew what and how to order, which spared us from the embarrassment and tongue-in-cheek humiliation that the place is known for.

We would stay this night at the Alford's residence in College Park, Georgia, near Woodward Academy, literally across the street from the school that the Alford children attended.

That evening Dean planned for him and me to go to watch his nephew's high school football game. This would be Dean's brother, Dan's, son's game. I also knew Dean's brother, Dan, from being a business partner in Dean's consulting business too, so I was excited that I'd get to see Dan on our visit also. We would leave shortly.

"The phone's for you, Dean," Terre called.

As Dean got the phone, Terre explained to us that the call was regarding a major Miracle League fundraiser event. Dean was in charge.

"Dean is involved in so many things. I don't know how he does it, but this is really special."

For Dean, a day off means never being more than one foot from his cell phone or a land- line, and he was on it often.

"What's the Miracle League?" I asked Terre.

"It's a baseball program for handicapped children that Dean and his Rotary Club started. It is played on a rubber surface field. They raised a million dollars. They built this field...Dean can tell you about it," Terre responded.

When Dean got off of the phone, I asked him more about the Miracle League. He told me about his Rotary Club starting the program and how they built the first rubber surface field. He mentioned the big league Atlanta Braves players and other celebrities that were involved. The first field was built in Conyers, Georgia. The idea took off so well in the Atlanta area that several others were soon built.

The question entered my mind about how you could justify a dedicated field for just children with disabilities.

"That's a question we get all of the time," Dean said.

Dean knows about my health. Hearing about his accomplishments for children with disabilities peaked my interest. I listened closely.

He told me about how there are 5.2 million children in this country with some form of disability. When you count all forms of learning disabilities in this count, 1 in 5 in our local schools have some type of disability. Your town school district will be much the same. That's a huge population with a need for this type of entertainment. Little Leagues are selective. They have tryouts. Only one hundred or so will get selected to play, for which there will be a dedicated

Little League field. On the other hand, all 5.2 million children with developmental challenges are eligible to play Miracle League baseball, regardless of their capabilities. Surely, we can dedicate a special field for them.

Dean's dream would be to see a league in every community, and, he, in fact, started a national organization, staffed to help others replicate the Miracle League concept and create their own leagues. His goal is for starting at least five hundred leagues around the country in the next five years, and maybe go International as well.

I still just could not envision what these special rubber surface fields were like. Miniature? Rubber? Dedicated to just a handicapped league? Can it be used for anything else once it is surfaced?

"There is one of these fields nearby the high school where the football game is tonight. I'll drive by there and show it to you," he exclaimed.

So, off to the football game we went, me asking Dean more questions about the program as we drove.

After the game, we returned home and Dean forgot about driving by the Miracle League field to show me. I didn't remember either. It was late, too late to go back. Tomorrow we would be going to the Georgia Tech football game.

Along came Saturday. It was college game day, a real treat I had been looking forward to. Dean had a reserved parking spot below the stadium. No walking involved. Just get out of the car and into an elevator up to the skybox section. Georgia Tech stadium only seats about fifty thousand. Not a huge venue, by comparison to, say, Wisconsin's Camp Randall, but they have their traditions. There's the "Ramblin Wreck," the band, reserved "Club" seats on the fifty yard line, and, of course, sky boxes. We met some wonderful people in the skybox who were guests of the Alfords as well and had a chance to talk more with their children, Jacque and Chandler. The food and beverages were excellent. I couldn't help thinking and talking about the Miracle League, however. Everyone seemed to know something about Dean's quest for the development of the Miracle League.

Georgia Tech won the game that day, so it was a happy day at the Alford's as back at their house, Dean checked his e-mail and said that when he was done he would show me one of those video documentaries produced about the Miracle League that he had stored on his laptop computer.

"The Press has been good to us. It has given the League national attention, with news features being done by MSNBC, *Sports Illustrated*, and HBO. Celebrities like Matt Lauer, MSNBC, Bryant Gumbel, and Frank Deford, *Sports Illustrated*, narrate the video features," Dean provided.

"The video tells the story better than I can describe it. We use them in presentations to groups. You can see the fields, the buddies, the kids at play, the faces and smiles of the kids and parents." He booted up his laptop and ran the video for me. He showed me the video done by MSNBC, Matt Lauer.

Dean went on to tell me more about the history of the league. He clicked on their web site and repeated the story as we read together.

"In 1997, the Rockdale, Georgia, Youth Baseball Association's coach, Eddie Bagwell, invited the first disabled child named Michael, to play baseball on his team; Michael a 7-year-old child in a wheelchair attended every game and practice, while cheering on his 5-year-old brother playing America's favorite pasttime."

In 1998, the Rockdale Youth Association formed the Miracle League to further its mission of providing opportunities for all children to play baseball, regardless of their abilities. The disabled children in the community had expressed the desire to dress in uniforms, make plays in the field, and round the bases just like their healthy peers. The league began with thirty- five players.

There were no programs for the Miracle League to copy. It was decided that:

- Every player would bat once each inning
- All players would be safe at the base
- Every player would score a run before the inning was over
- (last one up hits a home run)
- Community children and volunteers serve as "buddies" to assist players
- Each team and each player wins every game

The main concern was the playing surface, presenting potential safety hazards for players in wheelchairs and walkers.

So, in its spring of 1999 season, the Miracle League gained support and became a source of pride for all involved as participation grew to over fifty players. During that season, the magnitude of the need for such a program was recognized. It was learned that there are over 50,000-plus children in the Metro Atlanta area alone, who are disabled to some degree that keeps them from participating in team sports. That is when the dream of building a unique baseball complex for these special children was conceived.

The Rotary Clubs of Rockdale County, and Conyers, Georgia, where Dean is from, stepped forward to form the Rotary Miracle League Fund, Inc., a 501c3 organization. The new organization, he said, had two objectives, (1) raise the funds necessary to build a special complex with facilities that meet the unique needs of Miracle League players, and (2) assist in the outreach efforts for Miracle Leagues across the country.

With the help of community volunteers and companies, the design and construction of the first Miracle League complex was underway. The complex would include a custom-designed field with cushioned rubberized surface to help prevent injuries, wheelchair-accessible dugouts, and a completely flat surface to eliminate barriers to wheelchair-bound or visually impaired players. The design also included three grass fields, which could be converted to the synthetic rubber surface as the league grew. In addition, accessible restrooms, a concession stand, and picnic pavilion were included in the design.

That Miracle League complex was completed in April 2000. On opening day, the Miracle League rosters had grown to over one hundred players. By spring, 2002, over two hundred and fifty players were registered.

"Now I understand it!" I said.

The video was, in fact, as Dean said it would be, an excellent portrayal of the program that answered the questions that I had. I was able to see the special facilities field that they talk about, the buddies in their roles, and above all, the smiles on the faces of those kids, and the happiness of those parents watching their children enjoy the sport of baseball. Having Dean read me the history really made it sink in what a special thing this was that had been accomplished.

I was hooked. I can relate to these children, I thought. This just might be something that I could do with my life. Maybe, maybe not. That film and story, however, inspired me to investigate this further.

Selling the Idea

The long weekend was over. We had a great time. On the flight home, I kept replaying that Miracle League video in my head and thought, "Wouldn't it be wonderful to have a program like that for the eligible children in the Green Bay area?" The "Miracle" is in the creation of the smiles on those kid's faces that I saw when they hit that baseball, and in the smiling, cheering parents who watched their son or daughter experience that joy. I could make that "Miracle" happen for the disabled children in our community.

I could do it. It would take a lot of effort, but I could do it. I was retired now. I would have time.

When we got home, Mary Jo and I talked about it some more. I knew that it would be a commitment and something that I wanted to do, but would Mary Jo support my doing it? Was it okay with her that this is what I would do in my retirement?

I asked Mary Jo for her approval, to which she said fine, if I felt well enough, and if that is something that I had a passion about doing. She was hesitant to say how much she could help me, however. She expressed that she had her charity work interests that she likes and remained dedicated to continuing them. Namely, she is responsible for the parish rummage sale each summer, which turns out to be a major fundraiser for our church. Mary Jo has done such a great job at this, and has grown it from year to year. Besides, even though I retired, she continues to work her job as Paraprofessional, teacher's aide, in the Green Bay School system. With summers off she wanted to do her church stuff.

My decision was to go for it. It was now November of 2005. I wanted to have a League up and running by the next summer.

First, I contacted the Miracle League office in Atlanta, headed by Dean Alford's sister, Diane Alford, National Executive Director, telling them of my interest to start a program in Green Bay. Dean's role now is National Chief Executive Officer and Chairman of the Board of the national organization. Diane was and still is very prompt and helpful to all that I would need. She immediately sent me a manual, which contained, among other things, a "How to Get Started" section. Later on, the manual would be useful as it contained the sample registration forms, the duties and responsibilities for coaches, umpires, and buddies, sample waiver forms, rules of the game, a blueprint and all necessary specifications for building a field, vendor information on where to buy the rubber surface for the fields, where to obtain liability insurance through the Miracle League, and promotional materials for recruiting players and for raising funds.

Next, I would need a sponsor and a place to play. I am a member of the Allouez Optimist Club and was immediate Past President at the time. Our club was sponsor for a park in the Village of Allouez (Al'-o-way), an adjoining suburb community of the City of Green Bay, which is named Optimist Park. We were, in fact, residents of Allouez for several years, before moving to the City of Green Bay's west side of the Fox River. As sponsor for the Park, our club financially supported the maintenance and additions to the playground and softball diamond there. Contrary to public opinion, this park, however, had been designated the year prior, as being the needed site for one of the Village's required drainage detention ponds. Because of that, no further improvements were added from our club's funds, the softball field that customarily accommodated adult leagues, was no longer scheduled for use, all in anticipation of the pond going in. Residents complained, but were told it was the only site, and was a done deal. The park, the playground, the softball diamond began to deteriorate from neglect and went unused.

All of that would change when the planners succumbed to the resident's opposition and changed their minds about locating the pond at the Optimist Park site. The pond would go elsewhere, thus making the facilities available once again. I thought, my Optimist Club is already a sponsor of Optimist Park, the park seems like it would be available to us to play on, and my Optimist Club would make good sponsor for the annual League fee.

I made a presentation to my Optimist Club about my desire to start a Miracle League, showing the video that Dean Alford had once shown me and which was now included in the manual for promotional uses like this. I, therefore, petitioned my Optimist Club with a proposal, that, if I could secure the use of Optimist Park ball field to start up a Miracle League program, would our club come up with the annual five hundred dollar fee? The answer was yes. We would call it The Allouez Optimists Miracle League of Green Bay.

I was scheduled for the agenda at the next available Village Board meeting to bring my request. The local newspaper, the Green Bay Press Gazette, picked up on the forthcoming agenda and contacted me for a short article about our plan to create a local league, similar to the one at Kenosha, Wisconsin, the only other Miracle League in the state at the time. I knew that we needed publicity and worked hard at it. This would be the first news article about us.

On February 7, 2006, I made a presentation to the Village of Allouez Board, showing the same MSNBC film, once again, to explain what the Miracle League entails. A tear in the eyes of more than one or two in the audience was noted when the lights came up after the video. Now that Optimist Park would no longer be used as a detention pond site, I was requesting not only permission to start up a league for handicapped children there, but to allow improvements to be made to build a special rubber surface field, if funds could be raised to do so. The decision was unanimous, on both counts, approval to use the field to start up a program *and* approval to build a rubber surface field there, if private funding could be secured. The agreement would be that the Miracle League wouldn't own the facilities, but could make improvements at the park and have the priority of use to accommodate our league schedule. The facilities must be open, otherwise, for public use.

I received accolades from board members for my plan. Audience members also applauded the effort. In fact, one resident in the audience stood up and commended the effort and offered to help. That was Aimee Pietrek, who with her husband Joe, became one of our founding board of directors and regularly helped out with registration on game days that first season. Joe and Aimee's service was greatly appreciated, especially that first year.

The idea was sold. We got the "go ahead" that we needed. It was only the beginning of the Making of a Miracle...League.

The original softball field. The new Home of the Miracle League.

Getting Started

With the place and the sponsor settled, now I would need to establish some type of organization, and recruit players and buddies. For a Board of Directors, Steve Seidl, a fellow Optimist member, stepped forth and volunteered to be on the Board. I am especially thankful to Steve as he led us with his financial advice.

It would be only natural that the Allouez Parks Director be involved. Brad Lange, the Parks Director, who is also an Optimist Club member, agreed to be a Board member.

Robin Raj, who works for the Wisconsin Department of Health and Family Services - Bureau of Developmental Disabilities Services, is a resident of Allouez living nearby the park, and who has an interest in seeing some special needs equipment improvement be made at that park, also volunteered to join the Board.

And, my life-long very best friend, Ray Kopish, Green Bay Chamber of Commerce, who is also on the Village of Allouez Board that approved the proposal, volunteered to be a Board member.

As mentioned earlier, Aimee and Joe Pietrek were the remaining Founding Board members. With the list of founding members for our Board complete, I could now finalize and send in the application form and the five hundred dollar fee to join the national association. I had my son, Nick, a graphic artist, make an addition of the words "Allouez Optimists Miracle League of Green Bay" to the artwork of the Miracle League logo for us. We were now officially a member of the Miracle League with our own logo.

The next task was to get the word out to parents and recruit players. Meanwhile, fellow Board members were thinking of the plan to raise money to build a field. Recruiting players would not be an easy task. With health privacy laws, the probable organizations that serve the special needs children could not give names of families with potentially eligible athletes. I also did not have any funds to speak of to work with for such things as mailings, brochures, and making copies. I did get some inquiries from that first article in the Press Gazette and I did make up an information brochure on my home computer to explain the proposed startup of the league in a question-and-answer format. I also made up a registration form, a liability waiver form, and a volunteer form.

I personally visited then with various health care organizations, such as the local Cerebral Palsy Center, Special Olympics, the local hospital that had a program for children with special health care needs. I could make a few extra copies of my information brochure, but all of these organizations graciously made copies of their own and did distribute my information to parents. This saved me the copy expense. I am extremely thankful to especially these aforementioned organizations.

I tried also to get the information in the schools for their special needs students, but the chain of command for this, i.e., being instructed to go through the Administrative Office, Special Ed Department Head for approval and then they would decide if they will pass it on, not allowing to go directly to special ed teachers, rarely got the information to anyone.

I tried a contact at the Syble Hopp School, a dedicated education facility for children with special needs in De Pere, but I guess that, at that time, they didn't really grasp the concept and the communication also went nowhere. Some schools, however, ignored my inquiries as if I were just another solicitor. In one case, the school special needs director told me that she would distribute the flyer, but I would need to send her four hundred copies, because, she said, they could not discriminately give it to just those with special needs. They'd send the flyer home with *all* students. Needless to say, the schools were not my most productive communication chain. Not in our program's infancy anyway. So much for my non-existent copy budget. I gave up concentrating on schools that first year.

It was getting to be about the month of March. I was targeting for an Opening Day of June 29th. Still no players signed up. I remember my phone call and discussion with Diane Alford, at the Miracle League office.

"Do you have any more suggestions on how to recruit players?" I asked. "What if I don't get enough participants for a league?"

Calmly Diane reassured me that the eligible population of prospects is greater than you think. I was doing all of the right things. If anything, the more publicity we can get, the better.

"Try to get yourself in the media," she would say. "It will come. It always does." Little did I know she would be right.

That's when Teresa Williams, now Teresa Anderson, came into the picture. She absolutely, positively, made my day. Teresa, a regional programs manager for Special Olympics back then, and with a special needs daughter, heard about the plans for a Miracle League through the Special Olympics office where I had brought my brochure. Teresa was then and is now, one of the hardest working and most dedicated accomplices for our program that there ever could be. She is currently our Vice President in charge of Volunteers, is a Coach, and is a new Board member. Teresa, as it turns out, was thinking of organizing a group of special needs children to play baseball together on a regular basis. She already had a group of twelve children ready to go. When she heard of the Miracle League, she decided to join us instead. We now had twelve recruits.

I would later contact Jeanette Brittain at my former work place, whom I knew had a special needs child, and also thought that she could help recruit other possible parents and volunteers she might know at Wisconsin Public Service. Jeanette had heard about the formation of the league from the Cerebral Palsy Center, but said that her son would be four years old and not five years as my original brochure eligibility indicated. So, I changed the age criteria to *four* years through nineteen years instead of *five* to nineteen. Jeanette then did sign up her son, Evan. Now our total was up to thirteen players.

For additional recruitment methods and ideas, I contacted my friend and old high school classmate, Tom Dallman. Tom and his wife, Cheri Long, Green Bay, were both social workers at one time, are now both retired, and have cared for an adult man, named Lawrence, in their home for several years. I thought Tom might have some ideas on communication channels. Tom himself suffers from a neurological disorder, which affects his balance. He has been retired for some time. Tom knew of some contacts we could make, but most were organizations that accommodate adult special needs, not children, like ASPIRO, and NEW Curative. We chatted. Then Tom said, "That is a wonderful thing you are working on. You'll need some seed money. I'm going to send you five hundred dollars."

Wow! Five hundred dollars! I now had some operating money. I had been going to Kinko's for making copies and sending faxes. With the money I would buy a printer-copier-fax machine. Now I could make my own copies at home. Tom and Cheri have a Charitable Foundation and have gone on to continue to support the Miracle League in subsequent years. They have furnished me with a digital camera with which many, many action photos for our web site and numerous presentations I have given have been taken. Tom also originally set up a gift card at Camera Corner, so that there would be money to develop those photos. He suggested and purchased an Apple laptop for me for its superior photo management capabilities and generally to make my life easier in all the records and computer work I must do. This year, Tom and Cheri purchased a video projector for me for the numerous group presentations that I make. Cheri would further arrange for me to make a request to her father's foundation. A multi-year pledge from the Don Long Family Foundation was the result. So, needless to say, Tom and Cheri are some special people to me.

In addition to Tom and Cheri's five hundred dollars, another friend and high school classmate, Mike Audit, donated one hundred and fifty dollars to the cause for my seed money fund. I also contacted my friend and fellow Optimist Club member, Pat Murphy, who has always been generous in support of other projects that I have been involved with in the past. He gave one hundred dollars.

"It is a wonderful thing you are doing," Pat Murphy also would say. The truth be known, however, is that Pat really thought that this program was a lofty goal and didn't really think that it was something that I could accomplish. Nevertheless, today, when I see Pat, he wholeheatedly always compliments me and retells the story of how he didn't think that I would succeed in the plan.

Since I was an Optimist Club member, I wrote to the twelve local fellow Optimist Clubs, explaining the startup of the league and need for a startup fund, requesting three hundred dollars each. The Howard-Saumico Optimist Club, the Wednesday Noon Optimist Club of Green Bay, and the Sunrise Optimist Club of Green Bay were early responders that donated. I was so fortunate and grateful. This was how those initial expenses were met.

Meanwhile, my thoughts bounced back to what it would take to raise money and build our own field. According to the manual provided by the association, typical cost estimates for the construction of a rubber surface field range in the area of two hundred and fifty thousand dollars to four hundred and fifty thousand dollars. Diane Alford at the League office said that most typically the target to raise is four hundred and fifty thousand dollars for their construction. But, since in our case, we wouldn't actually own the land that it is on, our estimate more nearly approximated two hundred and fifty thousand dollars. I looked at the detailed breakdown of the items making up the estimate and two hundred and fifty thousand dollars seemed reasonable. So we established a campaign target goal of two hundred and fifty thousand dollars. My personal wish was, that, if we started up the league that first year, we would at least have the rubber surface field ready for the second season.

We would later file for, and our organization itself is now, a 501c3 tax-exempt, nonprofit organization. But for quick fundraising, since our Optimist Club already had a Foundation held by the Greater Green Bay Community Foundation, Inc., we could set up a separate fund within that Foundation. This would essentially be a nonprofit, community project fund. Steve Seidl and I, therefore, met with the Greater Green Bay Community Foundation and established the "Allouez Optimist Foundation Miracle League Fund." Donations to it would be tax deductible to the donor. The papers setting up the fund for the project actually serve as our organizational founding document.

Steve Seidl convinced me that we should contract with the Greater Green Bay Community Foundation for steering our fundraising campaign. Was that ever good advice, versus trying to save money and fundraise on our own! After all, the Foundation manages the philanthropic giving of many of the probable people we would have to search out on our own. Steve, a successful real estate and commercial property broker/owner, knows everybody and anybody in the community. When it came to assembling a fundraising committee, Steve pulled in some top names to help our cause. Steve was the key man. Our committee consisted of some Optimist Club members and some business people who are very well known in the community.

Fundraising Committee:

- Myself, Paul Liegeois – Retired, Wisconsin Public Service; Chair of League Board; Member of Allouez Optimist Club
- Steve Seidl – Broker/Owner – Seidl & Associates; League Board Member; Member Allouez Optimists
- Ray Kopish – Vice-President – Green Bay Chamber of Commerce; Allouez Village Board
- Gary Ziegelbauer – President/Owner – Miller Distributing
- Jim Ritchay - Vice-President- Smith Barney; Member of Allouez Optimists
- Lori Stein – New York Life Insurance Co.; Member of Allouez Optimists
- Michael Frohna – Bellin Foundation; Member of Allouez Optimists
- Laura Mossakowski – Owner – Laura Mossakowski Financial; Member of Allouez Optimists

If some of the high profile people that Steve contacted would not be active committee members, they either agreed to attend one of our meetings to give advice, give us additional contact names, or make a pre-promotional call to one of our prospects that they would know to pre-recommend our project before we visited that prospect. Among this type of advisors were:

- Tom Olson – Retired President of U.S. Paper; Attorney
- Rick Chernick – President/Owner – Camera Corner Connecting Point
- John Hickey – Cornerstone Foundation

- Dan Gulling - Retired President of Marinette Marine Corp.

The Greater Green Bay Community Foundation provided us with a list of probable foundations and individuals whose giving criteria are known to match our project. This list became our targets. We would purchase a few personal, portable DVD players for personal showing of the Miracle League video when funds proposals would be made. This was an excellent tool. If you could get a prospect to view it, the success rate in getting a donation was quite high…very, very few rejections.

Recruiting for both players and buddies was coming along. It was by a stroke of luck however, that a week or so after my presentation to the Allouez Village Board, reporter, Mike Hoeft, from the Green Bay Press Gazette, who just happened to be there that night at the meeting to cover a totally different topic, a controversial plan for installing the Village's first roadway "roundabout," saw my presentation and called me. He wanted to do a story and asked if I could get some of the kids together playing baseball for a photo.

Teresa Anderson was able to arrange the kids from her group to come to Allouez Optimist Park for some practice and photos. The next morning the story appeared in the newspaper, on April 25, 2006, front page, color photo of one of our players, Austin Drew, ten years old, who has Down's syndrome. The photo was excellent, with baseball cap on and ball in hand, intent and ready to throw a pitch.

Drew's mom e-mailed me, delighted at the photo. "Isn't he handsome?" she wrote.

And handsome he was. Drew was the man of the day at his school that day. My phone rang off the hook, and e-mails bombarded my computer as soon as the paper hit the morning delivery boxes. This would be *the* single most significant turning point for our success to date. Registrations rolled in, volunteers inquired, donations and player sponsorships were received.

We were just getting started.

The Green Bay Press Gazette, front page, 4-25-2006
(Reproduced with permission from the Green Bay Press Gazette)

Play Ball!

We had sixty-five players on four teams that first season. Allowing time for ordering of uniforms and volunteer T-shirts, printing of sponsor names on the backs, purchase of insurance, and recruitment of the necessary volunteers for buddies, an opening day for the season was set for a Saturday, June 29, 2006. This is later in June than our normal schedule today. All four teams would play that day. I had otherwise set a schedule where we would have one game on Tuesdays and one game on Thursdays at 6:00 PM, so that each team would play one game per week and late enough so parents could get there on time from their work. We would play for six weeks that first year.

As typifies the kind of children that would join the League, there was 9-year-old Megan Vincent. Megan arrived at the ballpark in her brand new three-wheel walker, pushed by her mom. Her mom, Connie Rissling, who was proud to have her daughter be part of a team for the first time in her life and proud to say that she "had to go to her daughter's ballgame today" also typifies the joy that this program has brought to the parents. Megan had cerebral palsy. That three-wheeler, Connie said, cost nearly as much as the car she was driving. Connie did not have extravagant financial resources by any means. But, Megan needed that three-wheeler for baseball, she said. She sacrificed.

Megan's team that first year was the Mariners. She was smartly dressed in her new team jersey and new hat. Her mom had sewn on her Miracle League arm patch.

In her first at-bat, with mom as her buddy, mom would hold Megan's head upright and help her hold the bat, as they took their position in the batter's box at home plate. With one mighty swing,

24

mom, of course, assisting, the bat hit the ball off of the tee for a base hit. A beaming smile by the child is always the result of making contact with the bat on the ball. "Running" the bases was accomplished by mom pushing that three-wheeler around the basepaths, until it was her turn to score a run. It was hot that summer and you could see mom work up a sweat in her pushing duties as "buddy" for Megan.

With Megan now on third base, as the batter at the plate hit the ball, Megan, with mom pushing again, "ran" towards home plate to score a run. Megan would do the "running" motion with her dangling legs. To the sound of "Safe" called by the umpire, and to the announcement of her name being called for having scored a run, and with fans cheering her on, a beaming smile was again produced. The scenario would repeat itself child after child.

Like so many of the children with varying health conditions, especially the non-verbal or the wheelchair bound, like Megan, it is sometimes hard for an outsider to interpret their feelings and emotions, and to communicate with them. The parents, however, know their child's every mood. They know when that child is happy, grumpy, sleepy, or whatever. They know what their child is communicating. But a smile is a smile. I could aways interpret that. For children, like Megan and others, I had learned to just talk to them. They hear you and comprehend, in most cases, just perfectly. When a smile is the response, I know that I've made a positive connection with that child. You can't help but become attached to these kids.

There are costs to running a league. It costs about thirty dollars for a major league look-alike jersey and baseball cap printed with sponsor name and numbers added, and about eight dollars on average for player insurance. Parents need to sew on a Miracle League patch on the jersey sleeve. We would charge forty-five dollars as a registration fee to cover the average basic needs cost per participant.

It is our goal that no player be turned away due to inability to pay. Our experience would be that about twenty five percent of parents would need assistance with the fee. To this, add that we would need liability, and errors and omissions insurance for the volunteers and Board of Directors, and uniforms and hats for the Head Coach and Assistant Coaches, which I didn't expect them to pay for. My dream was to make this as memorable of an experience for each child as possible. I describe it as wanting there always to be a "Disney World" atmosphere for these kids. So, I had hoped that we would be able to provide free team photos for each child, trophies at the end of the season, and I envisioned having some sort of cost-free special Family Celebration event at the close of the season. We would also need equipment, I thought. For these additional costs I would seek sponsors.

It would not be difficult to recruit Team Sponsors. By now, with the front-page newspaper exposure that we received, the public was a little knowledgeable of our program plans. A team sponsorship was set at five hundred dollars. For establishing sponsor fee levels, by the way, I had consulted with Diane Alford at the League office, who was always helpful in giving me advice on what others were charging and pointing out other areas that may be potential for sponsor income opportunities.

One team sponsor, members of our Optimist Club, came forth immediately. Business partners, Laura Mossakowski and Al Naumann would sponsor the Allaura Financial Solutions Red Sox. We had one sponsor. Another sponsor from our Optimist Club, Larry Barton, was recruited and agreed to be a sponsor. His team would be the Edward Jones Investments – Larry Barton, Financial Advisor Mariners. We had two. A third had contacted me by e-mail, interested in being a team sponsor. The third original team would be the Max & Erma's Indians, Lisa Muller, owner at the time. We had three. For the fourth, I visited with my friend and local manager at the Dodge Dealership, Scott Borths. They agreed right away. The fourth team would be the Gandrud – Chevrolet Chrysler Nissan Dodge Brewers. We had our team sponsors. I would need a sponsor to be able to purchase Miracle League T-shirts for the buddies.

For the volunteers' shirts sponsor, Teresa Anderson's friend with a real estate business had indicated that he would help in some way. Just contact him, he said, which I did. The fee was five hundred dollars. I am very grateful to Tom Monahan and Resource One Realty. They have been repeat sponsors of volunteer shirts each year since that first season. This first year I would purchase as many shirts as five hundred dollars would buy, taking into account that there would be some cost to print a "Resource One Realty" logo on the backs. Team Apparel

& Specialty Co, in Green Bay has regularly given us a discount on screen-printing for all of our shirts and jerseys, as well as cut the price on trophies we purchase. So, that first year we had seventy-five "Angels in the Outfield," Miracle League T-Shirts, which would be issued to the volunteers as the official buddy shirts.

Individual contributions toward scholarships additionally helped defray the costs for those unable to pay.

We played on the existing dirt field that year. Players like Megan Vincent, had a difficult time in the dirt with their walking devices. I so admired the courageousness of her mom to always be there to plow the way through that field for Megan.

To try to make the field conditions as smooth as possible, I sought the help of friends who helped me groom that field before our season. After all, that facility was not being used and was neglected. We pulled weeds, raked and leveled the infield, and applied weed killer around the fencing to spruce the area up. There was no electricity, water or bathrooms, and no shade for the kids, just a few in-the-ground benches that served as dugouts. The Parks Department furnished a wheelchair accessible port-a-potty. They would also apply fresh new chalk on the foul lines in prep for our games. There was a locking wood storage box that we were allowed to store our equipment in on-site. The grass was kept cut for us. Brad Lange and the Village of Allouez Parks & Recreation Department have been wonderful to us from day one.

We would need some baseball equipment, but that would not turn out to be a problem. A supply of used helmets, bats, and catcher's masks was offered to us by the DePere Girls Softball League. Several groups and individuals gave us bats and gloves. I did need to purchase balls, a soft rubber baseball, and a catcher's mask. I also purchased an official blue umpire's shirt to dress the umpire in. For the umpire's hat, I just used a blue baseball hat that I had and sewed a Miracle League arm patch over the hat's old emblem. That was it as far as equipment needed to get us started.

Theresa Drew, mom of Austin Drew, volunteered to help with the scheduling of buddies. Buddies, or "Angels in the Outfield" are able-bodied persons, twelve years old or older, who are assigned to each player to assist with batting, fielding, and "running" the bases as much or as little as that player needs. Buddies can be friends, neighbors, parents, siblings, or just those willing to volunteer their time. Ideally, a non-related buddy is preferred, as it gives a chance for the player to become acquinted with a new friend. Oftentimes, a friendship develops. Buddies become more enlightened and accommodating to lives of people with special needs too.

I like to tell the story about the buddy that contacted me by e-mail at Christmas time and asked, "Can you give me the address of Michael, for whom I was buddy this year? I'd like to send him a Christmas card."

I looked up Michael's address right then and responded. In the meantime, an e-mail came back saying, "Thank you for your prompt reponse with Michael's address. But just by coincidence, in today's mail, *I* received a card from *him!*" How neat. So, lasting relationships do happen in the Miracle League.

By now I have amassed a huge list of names and contact information of people that had called me by phone or e-mailed me about being a buddy. I have multiple spreadsheets that I keep on my PC; the player registration, the financial accounting, the list of potential volunteers names, and my list of every other contact person that I would need to keep. There were additional prospect names that others and I just randomly thought of in case we wouldn't get enough volunteers. Theresa would have to call or otherwise contact this list of people and schedule them.

Buddies were matched with players according to the preference indicated by the parent of the child on their registration form. Theresa developed a schedule for the season. I am very appreciative of Theresa's help that first year. It was a learning experience. Buddy scheduling each game is a challenge.

An information meeting was held at the Allouez Village Hall for parents to explain the program and what to expect. I showed the video as a visual explanation of what it would be like. Again, you could see tears being held back here and there after the viewing. It was there that the additional coaches, assistant coaches and team moms came forth. Teresa Anderson and her group of children she brought would be one coach and one of the teams.

Another meeting was held for training and information for the volunteers. I invited someone from the Cerebral Palsy Center to talk a little with the buddies with advice on assisting those with special needs. The best advice was to visit with the parent prior to the start of a game and learn each child's situation individually.

I held a Coaches' "Draft" after the registration deadline was done. We do this each year. At the draft, players were placed on teams, trying to evenly distribute by age, disability, and honor any special parent requests, like ride share, or friends that want to be together.

I wanted the complete package of what the Miracle League should be, including a public address announcer who would call out the names of kids when they come to bat. As I understood from the pointers in the League manual these kids love to hear their name called and sound was part of the ambience. I wanted it for the "Disney World" effect; remember. I wanted sound. There was no electricity at the field, however. So, at the parents meeting I mentioned all of this and said that we would need a portable electric generator. I asked if anybody had one that we could use. Three dads came up after the meeting and said that they had a generator we could use. I had the electricity we needed. Bob Mottl would bring his Honda generator for each game for us to use.

I had portable electricity now, but no sound system yet. I remembered my friend, Bruce Vanden Plas from the Southwest High School baseball program, mentioning that they got a new public address system for the Southwest High School baseball field. I contacted Bruce to find out what happened to the old system. It turns out that I could not only borrow the old equipment, but that we could keep it. Bruce donated that sound equipment to our League.

I had sound, a 500-watt amp/mixer and two large public address speakers. One of the dads came forward and said that he had sound equipment, too, and that he would be our public address announcer for as many games as he could make. Doug Phillips is a wedding-type DJ as a sideline job, and had all of the sound equipment as well as music we would need. His wife, Jan Phillips, was already one of our coaches for daughter, Carley's team. The equipment from Bruce Vanden Plas then would be needed as backup and for games where

Doug could not attend. I would, of course, need another DJ, for which I recruited my brother Leo Liegeois, as the alternate. So we had the sound system worked out. I just hoped that it would work okay on a portable generator.

Storing all of this equipment by the way, the large bags of bats and helmets and now the sound system, would not be a problem. Brad Lange let us store it at the Village Hall which is only about two blocks away from the park. Other Village recreation program equipment, like for the Little League, was stored at the Village Hall too. So, I at least did not have to keep this stuff at my home for the winter.

I wanted the inaugural opening day to be special. The Miracle League manual had some case history examples of some things that other members have done for their grand opening. Playing the national anthem was the first thing that was, of course, customary for the league. I would not only have the national anthem, but had a singer.

I would also arrange for the U.S. Marines to be present. The local Marine office honored my request. At the opening event the Marine Color Guard, consisting of four Marines in their dress uniforms, marched onto the field carrying the U.S. flag and the Marine flag, marched to home plate, then up to the pitcher's mound, where they did an about face and turned to the crowd for the national anthem. They were awesome! The players and their buddies would be asked to come onto the field and line up on their respective baselines. Having the national anthem and players lining up on the baselines became a tradition continued at all games. For our regular games I would recruit two people to march out to second base, unfurl and hold up the flag between them, a five foot by eight foot flag that I personally brought each time from home. The two would then end this little ceremony by folding the flag back up and marching off the field. That opening season we did not have a flagpole, so this is how we did our national anthems.

I was the MC. It was show time. I got there very early. So did Doug Phillips, our volunteer soundman. Doug set up his sound system and carted his huge speakers to their locations on the grass on either side of the existing six-tier bleachers behind home plate.

"Would the portable generator work?" we thought. "Would it have enough power? Would it blow a fuse?"

We started up the generator. He set up his amplifier on a folding table just outside of the backstop fence to the first base side of the field. Except for the noise of the gas engine on the generator the sound system worked great. We would take a long extension cord and place that generator farther away from the crowd to muffle the engine noise, but we were in business. Doug and I tested out the microphones and his selection of music. As a wedding DJ he had a case full of music CD's. He also had a cordless microphone that I and the singer for the national anthem would use out on the field by the pitcher's mound for the ceremony while he used a corded mic. Just as a backup, we made sure that the corded microphone cord was long enough to push through the fence and stretch all the way to the pitcher's mound, in the event that the cordless microphone didn't work. Everything worked flawlessly. I was elated. We'd have to remember to always have gasoline there, as the engine would require refueling a few times each game.

For an opening ceremony I included a big "Thank You" to the Village of Allouez and invited the Village President to say a few words. Patricia O'Neal, Village President, commended all those who had a part in bringing youth baseball to this very special sector of children with special needs. She said it was a welcome addition to Allouez and looked forward to working with us on expansion.

Beforehand, I had wanted to invite and have present, local area athletes that, either now or in the past had played baseball in the big leagues, or at least get letters of commendation to read. I was successful in getting such a letter from Bob Wickman, an Abrams, Wisconsin native and, at that time, an active pitcher with the Cleveland Indians. Bob Wickman was, in fact, selected for the years 2000 and 2005 Major League All-Stars. I got this "Congratulations" letter signed by him and sent with a signed baseball card, by way of contacting his mom.

I read other similar "Congratulations"-type letters for our opening day from Casey Kopitzke, De Pere native who was playing for the Des Moines Cubs farm team and whose wife I would get in touch with here in town, Jack Tashner, UW-Oshkosh and friend of Casey's who pitches for the Giants, and Tim Jorgenson, who lives in the area, works at Associated Bank and played at one time for Cleveland. I read those cards and letters of inspiration on that opening day. Tim Jorgenson has since joined our Board of Directors.

Also in attendance was John Gard and his wife Kate. John was a State Representative and Speaker of the House at the time. He was also a candidate for Congressman. I was honored to have him there.

To throw out the first ever, first pitch, I chose a young man with cerebral palsy and in a wheelchair, Ryan Blashka, from Two Rivers, Wisconsin, whose mom, Connie, was the first parent to contact me about playing in the league. Ryan was twenty-three years old and beyond our age limit, but even though he could not play, I invited him and his mom to the opening for being first. Turns out that I had an extra Brewers team jersey and hat that I gave to Ryan to wear that day and keep. I ordered a special Miracle League logo baseball for that day, as the one Ryan would throw out so he could keep that too as a memento. And so, the ceremony concluded with my introducing Ryan and the reason he was chosen to throw out the first pitch. They stuck around to watch the games. Ryan asked me to sign his baseball for him and wanted a picture with him and me together. His mom would stay in touch by e-mail and would later help distribute my information flyers in the Manitowoc/Two Rivers area. She said that Ryan has his jersey and hat proudly displayed and hanging on the wall in his room.

I knew the value of getting media coverage. Just look at what that one front-page newspaper article did for us. So, I tried to work through any connections and contacts that I knew at the local TV stations to inform them of our league's inaugural opening day and invite them. At TV-5, my good friend and also a high school classmate, Dan Popkey's son Ryan Popkey, was the Sports Reporter. I e-mailed my news release to Ryan. I also called his dad about my desire to have Ryan cover the event in hopes that he'd talk to Ryan. I even stopped by the TV-5 studio to pay a visit to Ryan.

I similarly contacted TV-2, directing my news release to the news anchorman and former sports announcer, Bill Jartz, whom I knew personally. He responded to my e-mail immediately and said that he would pass it on. Likewise, TV-11 was contacted. So was the Press Gazette, where I now had a contact with the Allouez beat reporter, Lee Reinsch. Not to worry. All three of those TV networks and the newspaper were there that day to cover the opening. In fact, Ryan Popkey further did a longer version feature about the program for his late-night, after-the-news feature, *"Sports Extra."* We had another color picture and front page of the paper the next day.

Now I'm not afraid of getting in front of the camera on TV. Everyone's a little nervous when it comes to that. I had some experience in public speaking as part my job at Public Service in the many years in Marketing. But I knew that there would be the probability of interviews on TV and it would be me that they would want to talk to. So I was prepared. I could ask them to speak to someone else, but bad or good at it, I was the one that needed to talk. It would be just the real me, I thought.

My father, Bill Liegeois, was a TV and radio personality. Back in the 1950's when I was a child, my dad was the first news, weather, and sports person for Channel 11 TV. The station was located in Marinette, Wisconsin. Later, TV-11 would be moved to Green Bay, where my dad chose not to move, but to stay in Marinette on the radio as DJ and local sports announcer at radio station WMAM. He passed away in 1982 at the early age of fifty-nine from cancer. I know that dad would have no problem with interviews, but that doesn't mean his talents rubbed off on me. He would be proud of me. We needed the publicity and I knew that I needed to be a spokesperson.

The kids were a little timid at first, a new activity, loud noises and a loudspeaker calling out their name, and cheering for them. All players bat every inning. Once they got the hang of it you could see them loosen up and enjoy the game. Like 10-year-old, developmentally delayed, Tyler Bix from Howard, Wisconsin. By his second at-bat, after his name was called he approached home plate, took his position in the batter's box, tapped home plate with his bat. He then raised and pointed his bat Babe Ruth style. Only he would not point to the outfield, but rather turned around, facing all of the parents on the bleachers behind home plate, and with bat pointing in air, proclaimed, "This one's for you, mom!"

Then there was 9-year-old Jacob Vanden Berg who is cognitively delayed, non-verbal, and mostly grunts to communicate. Jacob was one of those who was a little timid at his first at-bat, but by the second inning, after watching it all take place, when he came to bat, he stood in the on-deck circle and waited his turn. The public address announcer was playing music between innings and was behind on calling the names for the next inning. Jacob would not budge out of that on-deck circle. He grunted. Turns out, he now knew the routine and was not going to move, until his name was announced. I could tell that the kids were having fun.

A few games into the season, another mom, Linda Kemper, asked if she could bring some snacks and soda to sell at the games. She said that she had recruited another mom, Wanda Sperry, who would help her. They purchased some items and soda to sell. They even got some things donated from Shopko, and Larry's Piggly Wiggly in De Pere. And so our concession stand was started. Linda would back in to the gravel parking lot, up onto the grass, and sell those treats and sodas out of the back of her van. She would be at each game, either her or Wanda. Later I purchased some Miracle League hats from the league, which they sold for ten dollars each. The hats were a hot commodity. I wish that I would have purchased more of them to sell. They sold out right away. Again, I didn't have much money to work with at that time. With the donated goods and great sales, we netted four hundred dollars from Linda's concession stand that first year. Thank you to Linda Kemper and Wanda Sperry.

Each team would have a team mom. Team moms would arrange a schedule for bringing a team drink and snack for after every game.

Our fundraising was underway and throughout the season I would announce our plans to build a special rubber surface field with hopes to be ready for the next year of the program. I typed up and posted on the backstop fence an updated donors list at each game. You could check our progress.

In the Miracle League, remember, every child bats every inning, every child gets a hit, every child scores a run, last batter up hits a home run. There are no outs. My favorite spot to take photos is looking down the first base line at home plate and snapping a picture of the kids when they get a hit. The smiles beam from ear to ear every time that ball hits the bat. I can see a moment of happiness on the faces of each child. I try to capture it in pictures. I used my new camera to take pictures at the games, then develop them and have them in an album at the next game. That first season I took tons of photos. In subsequent years, my son, Beau, would sometimes take those pictures, and other times, his friend, Michele Lemmens, would take them for me. The photos would also help me put together video presentations that I would be asked to make to groups. Parents were free to take any photo that they liked, and they did.

We had Picture Day. Donn Bramer from Donn Bramer Photography, was interested in sponsoring Teresa Anderson's team that year, but that sponsorship was taken. He then inquired about taking our team photos for us, but I had given preference for this to another player's dad, who was a photographer at Ambrosius Studios, in Green Bay. As I mentioned, it was my intention to be able to provide a team photo to each family at no charge. Ambrosius Studio gave us a substantial discount, and also gave me extra copies for myself to keep and copy each for our team sponsors at no cost. Even though he wasn't taking the team photos, Donn Bramer still donated five hundred dollars and sponsored the trophies at season end. I really appreciated what Donn had done. The following years I made sure that Donn Bramer Photography was the sponsor for Teresa's team. Donn would take action photos, like I had done, and make them available on his web site for parents. See www.bramerphoto.com in his Sports photos gallery under Miracle League.

For a Grande Finale that first year, we played once again on a Saturday, August 4th, 2006. We would have Awards and Family Fun Day. Food would be free for players and family members, but families had to sign up and obtain ticket in advance. To make things easy, we ordered McDonald's hamburgers for distributing. The nearby Allouez McDonald's gave us a discounted price. In addition Breyers Good Humor Co. furnished free ice cream treats for everyone. They loaned us a freezer to keep the ice cream cold, but I would need to transport it to the park on my trailer and arrange to use another dad's portable electric generator to run it. Our concession stand ladies had a busy day that day. Linda Kemper obtained potato chips for free, and pop at a discount. My sister-in-law, Sherry Steffel, sponsored the balance of the cost that we had for the Family Day food. Sherry and my wife, Mary Jo helped along with other moms to distribute the food after each game. Allouez Beer & Liquor, owned by my friends Ed and Mary Gerczak, filled our ice needs at no cost to us to keep the pop cold.

Just prior to handing out the family food, a short awards ceremony was held where each child's name was called to come out and receive a trophy at midfield where we wheeled out a trophy cart. Fellow Optimist Club members and Board members were asked to also join me and the respective coach from each team, to shake hands and distribute the trophies.

This is the part of the season that I take great pride in. It is the end of the season for the children. It is the culmination of a year of work for me. To see the joy, one last time, on each child's face as they receive an award for playing baseball, makes my heart pump all over again. They are the envy of their sibling brothers and sisters, if for only that moment, and they know it.

"Yes!" says one athlete as he high-fives me with a warm hard slap to the hands after receiving his trophy.

"Alright!" says another as he waves his trophy above his head to proudly display it for all to see.

Trystan Willems, a wheelchair bound boy and non-verbal, could not shout out his joy, but his eyes lit up and he smiled a big smile on receipt of his trophy.

For this game, we graciously were treated to guest baseball players from the nearby Appleton Timber Rattlers, a Seattle Mariners, Midwest League team, arranged by my friend and dentist, Rich Tonelli, who happens to be on the Rattlers Board. Wearing their team jerseys, they were introduced by me. They helped hand out trophies, and stuck around for autographs and photos. I have never seen so many wide eyes, smiles, and high-fives as these children receive a trophy for their efforts.

Just when I thought I was done handing out the last trophy to end the season, one of the player's moms, Amy Dahlin, and one of our Board members, Aimee Pietrek, came onto the field and surprised me when they took my microphone from me.

Amy Dahlin teared up as she read a "Thank You" certificate to me and gave me a big hug. The certificate was home made and signed by athletes, coaches and parents from that summer of 2006. It read,

"This certificate is awarded to: Paul Liegeois. This league is a dream come true for the players. Thank you for all of your hard work and dedication," signed... The Miracle League Players, Coaches, and Parents.

It is something that I cherish. Seeing Amy in tears made me choke up as well. This little thank-you gesture made me want to make things even bigger and better next year.

As the season wrapped up, Steve Seidl and I reminisced, with amazement, what progress that had been achieved to-date. Steve was such a tremendous help in all areas along the way, and still is. I couldn't help but wonder what motivated Steve to be so involved. So, I asked. He told me that he is happily remarried, but had a child with Down's syndrome, a son, by his first wife whom they had given up for adoption at birth. He had never seen nor heard from that son, nor did he know where he lived. He said, "I should have been doing this for *my* son."

Whether coincidence or a miracle of the Miracle League, shortly after hearing Steve tell me that story, Steve got a call from Madison, Wisconsin, tracking down the natural born parents of that son that Steve had not seen in nearly thirty years. The son had an illness and tests were needed from his parents. Steve traveled to Madison, where he not only provided the medical request, but also was reunited with his son. Steve learned of the son's past, and where he was living. Steve has gone on to regularly visit his son.

Our first season was a memorable one. Although we now have such wonderful new facilities, that first season will always be something special.

Doug Phillips, doing the DJ duties the first season in 2006.
Note the portable electric generator for power.
(Photo by Michele Lemmens)

Our method of flag ceremony and national anthem during our first year.

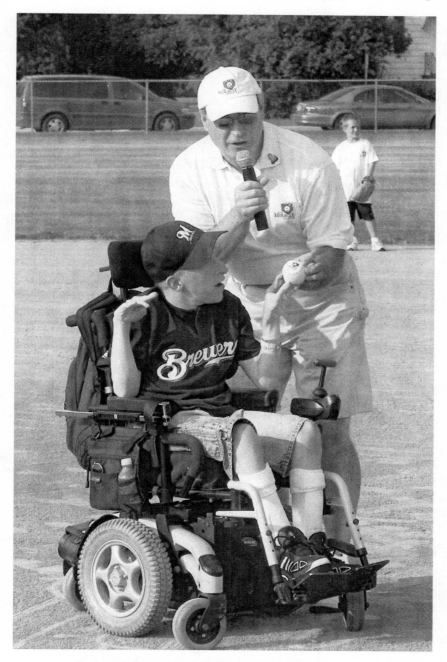

Ryan Blashka – First Pitch at first game in 2006.
(Photo by Michele Lemmens)

Adam Ehlers – First Year on the dirt surface field. Bob McCormik is the umpire. Michelle Ratchman is the "buddy" in the photo.

(Photo by Michele Lemmens)
Tyler Bix "This one's for you, mom!"

Paul Liegeois' father, Bill Liegeois, - Circa 1956, Marinette, WI, TV-11 Poster. He was an experienced public speaker.

Vision of What Could Be

The Green Bay Chamber of Commerce, in its publication, *BBJ* or *Bay Business Journal,* carried a feature on visioning. The feature was about local projects completed from vision to reality. For the cover they chose to depict the new Miracle League field with an action photo as viewed through a set of eye glasses, with the old dirt field in the background, to depict examples of community projects that had vision. The caption read, *"Visioning of What Could Be."*

My original vision was to see the construction of that new rubber surface field for the program, and to have it ready for the second season.

"That's it," I thought. If we could simply only build a field that would be ready for our next season. That's all I dreamed for.

I had set a dedication date for the start of our 2007 season of June 16, 2007. So everything targeted for getting constructed and done for June 16, 2007.

But the funds came so successfully that the "vision of what could be" would expand quickly to include the addition of a Bathroom/ Concession Stand/Storage Building, a great sound system, a paved parking lot, additions of handicap accessible playground equipment, and a walkway connecting everything throughout the park. We would even have electricity and water!

Fundraising would be quite successful, but the expansion of the dream was largely with thanks to major donors, Dick Resch and to Brett & Deanna Favre.

The Green Bay Chamber of Commerce, *Bay Business Journal* with cover photo illustrating a vision of the old and the new Miracle League baseball field.

(Reproduced with permission from the Green Bay Area Chamber of Commerce)

RAISING THE MONEY

Our fundraising committee met for the first time at the Greater Green Bay Community Foundation. Ken Strmiska, President of the Foundation, would lead us. He had a prospect list for us. He also recommended what to put into a presentation packet, like who we are, what our project goals are, the campaign budget, donor levels and what recognition, a pledge card, and pictures that support and help demonstrate by photos what the Miracle League program is about. We could add any other prospects we wanted, but Ken gave us a first priority contact list, second, etc. He always said that you needed an "ask" amount, so he furnished a dollar amount to ask for from each prospect. He said that it would help the project if you already had some donations toward your goal and could identify who has already contributed. I assembled the packets according to Ken's recommendation for our committee's use. We were still with limited funds so Steve Seidl offered to make several color copies at his office.

Our season was already underway, and there was already some TV and newspaper coverage, including coverage of our opening day. This was an advantage. Prospects, for the most part, had now heard something about the Miracle League. They knew we were for real. Our Committee would volunteer for who would make the contacts for the first priority list, especially if they had some relationship with the prospect. We each had copies of the Miracle League video to show.

First priority or not, I had already made my first presentation before our committee met. It was to Bernie Dahlin, owner of Nichols Paper Company. I knew Bernie, a very nice and generous man, who had supported a previous project that I was involved in. He contributed a large amount of money to get lights installed at Green Bay Southwest Baseball field back when my sons were playing ball. Bernie gave the initial contribution that got that project going. The Dahlin Family also was the naming rights donor for a new Southwest High School Football Stadium. It is named the Dahlin Family Stadium. This time I not only immediately thought of Bernie, but I knew that he had a personal interest. He had a grandson that was going to play in the league.

I had an appointment with Bernie at his office in Nichols, Wisconsin, about 20 miles from Green Bay, where his plant is located. I explained our program and project construction goals, then showed him the video on my personal DVD player. Bernie called me the next morning and pledged twenty five thousand dollars and immediately wrote the check for deposit in our Foundation project fund. We would now be able to tell other prospect donors that we had twenty five thousand dollars to date. I would add this contribution to the list that I displayed on the fence at our games.

Associated Bank donated five thousand dollars following my presentation to Bank President, Denis Hogan. Gary Ziegelbauer got twenty five thousand dollars from his friend, John Kress and the Kress Foundation at Green Bay Packaging Corporation. Steve Seidl contacted his friend Cort Condon, who is the attorney for the Dick Resch Foundation. Dick Resch is President, CEO, and majority owner of Krueger International, Inc, (KI) a contract office furniture company. His philanthropic giving already includes the Resch Center Arena, the Resch Aquatic Center, the Resch Olympic Pavilion, the Resch Trail, and many other causes, all here in the Green Bay area. Cort thought that our project met the criteria that Dick Resch would support and Cort would recommend that he contribute the naming rights level of one hundred thousand dollars.

Then came a call from one of our coaches, Steve Jossart. Steve's best friend, Mike Daniels, is President of Nicolet Bank in Green Bay. Mike Daniels is the contact for the Brett Favre Fourward Foundation. Deanna Favre is also on Nicolet Bank's Board of Directors. Steve Jossart would tell me that he told Mike what a great program that the Miracle League has been for his son. Steve urged Mike to recommend a donation from the Favre Foundation and told me that I should contact Mike.

I did call Mike. Between the contact with him, and through the Green Bay Packer's office representative for the Brett Favre Fourward Foundation, Aaron Popkey, the request for the support we needed was received. Aaron, whose brother Ryan I mentioned earlier, is also a son of my friend, Dan Popkey. Mike Daniels said that I didn't need to give him a presentation. He was already going to recommend a contribution at the one hundred thousand dollar level from the Favre Fourward Foundation. That was the naming rights level! Now we had two potential naming rights donors. We'd have to wait to see what materialized out of this, but things were looking pretty good, so we began getting real construction estimates.

I made another presentation to my former employer, Wisconsin Public Service and received a twenty-five thousand dollar pledge. I contacted my friend, Bill Ward, at Procter & Gamble locally here in Green Bay, who informed me how to go about applying for a grant on-line from their company. I should ask for twenty five thousand dollars, he said. He would recommend it. We received a check for twenty-five thousand dollars.

The Cloud Family Foundation gave twenty-five thousand dollars. The Schneider National Foundation gave twenty-five thousand dollars as well.

My friends Tom Dallman and Cheri Long, mentioned earlier, put me in touch with her Dad's foundation. I didn't need to make a presentation. They pledged twenty thousand dollars.

The Meng Family gave fifteen thousand dollars, Fred & Paula Schultz, ten thousand dollars, Schreiber Foods Employee Community Fund, ten thousand dollars, Paul Van Laanen, ten thousand dollars, Green Bay Home Medical Equipment, thirteen thousand dollars, all resulting from assigned contacts from our committee members, with those having a closer relationship with the potential donor volunteering to make the call.

Of course there were and continue to be many smaller donors from one dollar on up, some of which contribute annually.

A common theme of our success seems to be that friends do things for friends. Whether the friends that I contacted and whom graciously supported my cause did so out of sympathy for me, I will never know. It was apparent, however, that if a friend made the contact and proposal, they were more likely to support the cause of that friend.

CONSTRUCTION BEGINS

The Miracle League manual contained all of the specs we would need for building a Miracle League rubber surface field, including a blueprint for the excavation and gravel sub-base. The field consists of a rubber surface glued on an asphalt base, over compacted gravel. We would need to select a rubber surface vendor. There are different types of rubber surface that could be applied. The Miracle League had relationships with two vendors, that I was aware of, at the time. One sold a recycled rubber tile product, and another was a rubber carpet-type product. We had an estimate for the tiles. My wife and I visited the Kenosha, Wisconsin, Miracle League field to observe the tile product that they have installed, but we chose the rubber carpet from North American Specialty Flooring Company. We immediately signed on to an offer that they made to the first four Miracle Leagues to install their product at a special promotional price. The condition was that we install it that year.

Our estimated budget for the surface was one hundred and fifty thousand dollars. The surface would cost substantially less. Estimates were received for the excavation. This, too, was done for us at a substantial discount. The Village of Allouez would use its inventory of gravel and ground-up asphalt road tailings for the compacted sub-base of the field. So the field prep costs were less than budgeted. The same was true for the cost of the fencing, the bleachers, and the dugouts. Everyone was so generous.

With the prospect that we would have the Dick Resch donation of one hundred thousand dollars, *and* the Brett Favre Foundation one hundred thousand dollars, plus the pledges we had to-date, a Board meeting was held, and we decided to seek an architect to design a shelter in addition. We went ahead immediately with the field construction. It now was pretty apparent that we could go beyond my wildest dreams and build the shelter *and* the field.

It was now November of 2006. The surface vendor said that we'd need to wait 30 days after the asphalt is installed, before the rubber would be glued on. It was getting late in the year and cold for rubber installation, but we could do all the base and asphalt prep. We held a brief groundbreaking with our Board Members, the Village President, and any Village Trustees who could be present. The Village Parks Department then removed the old softball field fencing. Then we excavated and placed the asphalt that November. The asphalt was done and would cure all winter, much more than the requested thirty days, in hopes that the rubber surface would be installed as early as possible when it got warm enough in the spring. After all, we had still targeted for this all to be ready by June 16, 2007.

The architect for the shelter was from Foth & Van Dyke, again another high school classmate and friend was called upon, Neil Van Dyke. The shelter was designed, and one of Steve Seidl's companies, Superior Commercial Structures, Inc., (I've mentioned Steve before), offered to be the general contractor at cost. The architect concept that we came up with was estimated to be around one hundred and fifty thousand dollars. We thought that we would have about one hundred and twenty thousand dollars to spend, but still went ahead. The Village of Allouez required that the project be bid, which would cost us some lost time in our target, but the bid was done with written understanding that one bidder was offering to do it at cost. No other bids we submitted. Seidl was the general contractor.

We could still cut costs if subcontractors donated in-kind. So, I then made a contact to another friend who owns a mechanical firm, Tim Howald, Tweet-Garot Mechanical. Tim donated the plumbing and mechanical work for the shelter at his cost and donated the labor. This would save us six thousand dollars. The same went for the cement block, the flatwork, the electrical, and the sewer and water lateral extension contractors. When asked, they all reduced their estimates. We therefore, substantially reduced the shelter cost to within budget, and, provided the Favre and Resch money would materialize, we would be in good financial shape by spring.

I got the call we were waiting for from Cort Condon, Dick Resch's attorney. Steve Seidl and I were invited to Resch's office, where he completed and confirmed a one hundred thousand dollar pledge over three years for the project. He was first to put up the naming rights level contribution, thus the field would be named "Resch Miracle Field" at Allouez Optimists Park. I am so thankful to Mr. Resch.

In addition, although Mike Daniels, the Foundation Manager for Brett Favre, remained certain that the Favre's contribution would be the one hundred thousand dollars he recommended, we hadn't received it yet. He had talked to Deanna Favre. We had hoped that the timing would be so that the Favre's would receive naming rights to the field. Now Dick Resch had the field name, but Mike said that wasn't particularly important. The Favre's believed in the cause and wanted to support the project, he said. They would give one hundred thousand dollars anyway.

The Farve Foundation awards were made in December. I received a call from Mike Daniels to come and pick up the check. It was official! It was one hundred thousand dollars! It was two checks, actually, seventy-five thousand dollars from the Favre Foundation, the largest single contribution paid out by that foundation to-date, and a personal check for twenty-five thousand dollars. I immediately deposited the checks in our fund.

When I look back on it now, it almost seems like a miracle, in a way, that the funding for this project came forth so rapidly. Not only that, but there were two major donors right away. It was meant to be.

Because the Favres contribution was at the naming level, and because with that money we were able to exceed our goals, thus build a shelter with bathrooms, a concession stand, storage on-site, and a terrific sound system, we named the shelter and playground area in the Favre's honor. When consulting with Mike Daniels on what we should name this area, he said it wasn't necessary, but if we did, the Favre's would prefer something with Farve Family versus Brett Favre or Farvre Foundation in it. So, we named the area the "Favre Family Miracle Recreation Area." My son, Nick, the graphic artist, again helped design the sign for Favre Family Miracle Recreation Area.

In future years we plan to expand the handicap accessibility with additional playground equipment in the recreation area. Thank you, thank you, thank you to Brett and Deanna Favre.

I would have to appear before the Allouez Village Board with the Parks Director, Brad Lange, for approvals along the way, like approval to allow naming rights, approval of signs, and approval on the location of the shelter. The Board was extremely supportive.

I couldn't wait till spring. The snow was off the ground in April. Passers-by wondered what that asphalt parking lot-like pavement was for and why were we paving over the softball field. Construction for the shelter and the field began. The fence posts were installed and ready for the rubber surface crew. North American Specialty Flooring Company was ready to deliver and install the surface by the first week of May. Barring good weather, they said that it would take a week.

We needed to furnish three thousand bricks for them, which they used to hold the rubber carpet seams down when it is glued to the asphalt, and we could save ourselves some money if we made overnight arrangements for their crew. Brick pavers were donated to us by County Materials and would be saved to later put into a landscaped brick circle, where eventually we could sell commemorative engraved bricks. The Marriott Residence Inn, my friend, Jacqueline Smith, who is the Manager and is one of the Chamber of Commerce Ambassadors, gave us a substantial discount to house the crew. They loved it.

My friends at Eve's Supper Club in Allouez, where our Optimist Club meets, furnished me with discounted gift certificates for a good evening meal for that crew as well. The crew loved that too.

The weather cooperated. They completed the job in one week. The newspaper once again covered our project progress with two colored front-page features, one when the shelter construction began, and one when the crew was installing the rubber surface.

I visited the construction site daily. The project was on its way to meeting our completion target date.

Groundbreaking: From left to right, Robin Raj, Ray Kopish, Steve Seidl, Pat O'Neal, Paul Liegeois, Bill Sweasy, Joe Pietrek, and Brad Lange

Beginning of construction, November 2006.

The rubber surface being installed. The shelter under
construction in the background.   May 2007.

THE DEDICATION AND GRAND OPENING

It was close but the shelter was finished one week before the scheduled season opening day and dedication. We had enough funds to pave the parking lot, to pour a concrete walkway throughout the park from the parking lot to the field, to the shelter/concession stand, to the playground, and to the adjacent street. A wheelchair can navigate anywhere. All of this paving, and the installation of the signs was ready for our June 16, 2007, Dedication and Opening Day.

We thought that it would be a good idea to invite the neighbors surrounding the park to come for a tour and explanation of what goes on at a Miracle League game, prior to our grand opening. So, a door-to-door invitation was prepared and distributed by Robin Raj, one of our Board Members, who happens to live near the park. On an evening the week before the opening game, several of the neighbors showed up for a tour. I explained the Miracle League and took them all onto the field. I had the microphone on and used it so I could demonstrate the sound that they would hear around the neighborhood during games. Then we walked around to the concession stand and to the playground. I explained our future plans too. Some of these neighbors ended up volunteering as regular buddies and concession stand workers. There were no complaints voiced, only compliments.

I was fortunate to have special help with planning the Dedication festivities from a group of Leadership Green Bay (LGB) participants who chose the Miracle League for their project. Leadership Green Bay is a program for developing future leaders in area businesses put on by the Chamber of Commerce. Choosing a community project is a requirement of the training. Another of my sisters-in-law, Nancy Steffel, was part of the project team that asked if they could help the

Miracle League in any way for their project. We decided on help in promotion and recruitment for the Miracle League, and for planning the Dedication. The group consisted of:

- Nancy Steffel – Owner – The School That Comes to You, (English as a Second Language)
- Gary Rogaczewski – St. Vincent Hospital
- Randy Oswald – Wisconsin Public Service
- Tina Baeten – Family Services
- Jim Goetz – Chase Bank
- Joni Kolarik – Fox Communities Credit Union
- Mythili Nagarajan – Enzymatic Therapy Co.
- Patrick Blaney – Atty. Liebmann, Conway, Olejniczak & Jerry, S.C.

I met with this LGB team on a regular basis. They developed an informational brochure for me for the 2007 Season, and got it color printed at no cost, with Wisconsin Public Service doing the printing in-house and donating the copies for us. The group set out a promotion plan to recruit volunteers and players. I expected the 2007 season would have substantially more participants. I already had a waiting list. So, we would need more volunteers for buddies. The LGB group visited schools at their parent-teacher days; they contacted all of the area school administration offices and did a better job at this than I had been able to do on my own, created posters and placed them in businesses, grocery stores, the YMCA, got an announcement in their church bulletins, and published an ad in the Green Bay Volunteer Center booklet. The results were favorable as the 2007 Season had one hundred twenty players on ten teams, and now we had the numbers of volunteers needed as well.

I wanted the dedication to be something very special. This group was a godsend. We investigated what other Miracle Leagues had done for dedications and stole some ideas. As far as our planning for the Dedication Ceremony for the new field, the LGB group created a commemorative booklet with the Dedication agenda, which also served as a players' program, containing the rosters of all the teams, as well as a listing of all the donors. Again, one of the

LGB member's companies donated the printing cost. There would be a commemorative ticket made up. The naming rights donors were invited, Dick Resch, as well as the Favre's. We had to have the Village Board President invited and I asked Steve Seidl to represent our Board of Directors. In addition, all donors of over twenty five thousand dollars have their company logo painted on the surface of the field in the dugouts. They were invited, if they chose to be present, to sit on the field for the dedication. I also invited our Bishop of the Green Bay Catholic Diocese, Bishop David Zubick, to say a dedication prayer at the event. I personally made contacts with all of the local news media and invited them.

The LGB group arranged for mascot-type characters to be there, like Louie the Lightning Bug from Wisconsin Public Service, the Happy Joe's Pizza mascot, McGruff from the Police Department, Smokey the Bear from the DNR, and Sparkey from the Green Bay Fire Dept. They also got an air-driven "Fly Guy," it was called, the kind that is about 15 feet tall and which blowers inflate to make flap in the breeze.

I was contacted by a previous donor, who happens to work for the rescue helicopter service, who volunteered to have the Rescue III helicopter fly over after our national anthem. Imagine that, a flyover! We had a singer for the national anthem. The U.S. Marines attended once again, but this time they did not have colors to present, they had too many commitments that day and colors were not available, so our new flag would be hoisted on our new flagpole for the first time that day.

The LGB group was outstanding in their help that day. One of the members even built a balloon archway that the kids could come busting through as they ran onto the field to their positions for the first time. They made up reserved parking signs, they directed traffic, and blocked off a handicapped drop-off area. They staffed the area, allowing our special guests to park in the reserved spaces when they arrived. They helped out with player and buddy registration, they even helped staff the concession stand.

Our good friends, Barb and Fred Hoffman, let us borrow six red-white-and blue buntings, which were used to decorate the backstop.

The Hoffman's business, Home Interiors, was also a new sponsor of a team that year.

I also had the use of a podium from the Allouez Village Hall. We have a "Home of the Miracle League" banner that was used at our groundbreaking. We had to get Village permission to temporarily stretch and hang that "sign" high above on the backstop for the event. I wanted it up there, for at least the weekend after, when over fifteen thousand runners would be running by the park on the route of the annual world class Bellin (Health Care) 10K Run. It would be good advertising.

Everything was ready except the landscaped brick circle, about a 20-foot-in-diameter brick pavers circle, which was planned to be made from the used bricks. We therefore were not able to display a brass Dedication Day plaque that was made to be installed in the center of the brick circle. You can see the finished product, however, in the photos of this book.

It was finally Saturday, June 16th. I prayed for good weather once again. It was a perfect day. Everything was ready. I arrived at 5:00 AM, especially because I wanted to be sure that our sound system would work for the first time. We actually had a real concession stand. Linda Kemper and Wanda Sperry, the two moms who started the concession stand from the back of a truck, volunteered to run it again. They were in seventh heaven with the new facilities. I handled the soda ordering and delivery from Pepsi, and kept the cash box. They handled the rest. We had to buy a popcorn popper, a small used refrigerator, and a microwave. We kept the menu simple; hot dogs, popcorn, nachos, soda and snacks. On some days, Linda would cook up something special, like her "walking tacos".....mmmmmmmmm, nachos with meat sauce, peppers, and salsa. These got a little hard to keep, but, nonetheless, they were good.

The ceremony went well. I was the MC. My honored guests were seated around me at the podium at the pitcher's mound. All local TV stations were there. Even my good friend, Dean Alford from Atlanta, personally came for our ceremony. Someone estimated attendance to be over one thousand people. Several of my fellow Optimist Club members, like Nick Lanser, Gene Eggars, Lisa Kawala, Stu Goldman, Dave Jones, Mike Hagerty, and Dave Linz, to name a few, were there to help that day, too. If nothing else, they handed out the program booklets. Everything went as planned, except that we were expecting Deanna Favre and she was not there. Recall that I had a helicopter that would be doing a fly over and the spotter on the ground, who was in communication with the pilot, had told me that the chopper was in the air. Mike Daniels was there to accompany Deanna Favre and said that she was, in fact, on her way, but got hung up in traffic with an accident on the bridge. In the distance, I could see the helicopter hovering. I couldn't have it wait, so I began without Deanna.

The national anthem was sung, and, on que from the spotter, the helicopter flew towards me from the distance, and over our field, to the applause and cheers of all in attendance. It circled and then left.

Dick Resch, seated to my side at the podium, upon seeing the helicopter come toward us for the flyover, smiled, and chuckling, said to me "Wow, you really think of everything." That made me proud. It was so cool.

Laura Schmidt, a senior at Notre Dame Academy in Green Bay, who one of our Optimist members knew and arranged, sang the national anthem. Laura is the daughter of Dr. Frederick and Beth Schmidt, one of our contributors. Laura was so good. She had sung the national anthem before at other events, including at the Timber Rattlers minor league baseball games, and was a recipient of the prestigious Exemplary Award back in 2006 at the State High School Solo Ensemble. She now attends the University of Wisconsin, Eau Claire.

Deanna Favre pulled in to the parking lot. With all of the cheering and commotion temporarily at that moment from the flyover and return of the players from the baselines, where they were lined up for the national anthem to their dugouts, Deanna made her way onto the field and took her place among the seated guests, just as if her entrance was planned that way. After short comments by my honored guests, including Dick Resch and Deanna Favre, they were given Miracle League baseball hats, and individually given each a framed "Honorary Miracle League Buddy" Certificate, which we had made up, having a glass front and back so that on the back were all of the signatures in view of the athletes as a thank you. I even made up a special one for Brett Favre on the chance that he would be present as well. So, Deanna Favre was presented with her own certificate as well as one for Brett.

The formal part of my little ceremony concluded with all of the honored guests joining me at home plate where a ribbon cutting was done. The Green Bay Chamber of Commerce provided volunteer "Ambassadors" in their green sport coats, along with the ribbon and large ceremonial scissors.

I read the following dedication verse as our naming rights donors, Dick Resch and Deanna Favre, cut the ribbon,

"On this 16th day of June, 2007, we dedicate this baseball field as Resch Miracle Field and this special Miracle play area and shelter building as the Favre Family Miracle Recreation Area, so that a ALL children may have the opportunity to play baseball."

Then, I turned to the crowd and said "Now let's all join in singing *Take Me Out To The Ball Game.*

I glanced over to the public address announcer as if he should now play the music. He looked bewildered. One small problem, I included the words to the song in the player program booklet that was passed out to everyone in attendance so the could sing along, but I neglected to notify the public address announcer of the plan to sing it along *to music!* Not only that, I forgot to bring the CD with the music for that song on it. So, not having the music to play, I just asked everyone to follow me as I started singing the tune myself, *"Take Me Out To The Ballgame, Take Me........"* Immediately everyone joined in, the microphone was passed to the mouths of my singing guests. It turned out fine.

Deanna Favre was great. Her ceremony comments were so appropriate. She said that she and Brett were happy to be part of this program and that she and Brett have a place in their hearts for children with special needs. Brett's mom was a teacher for special needs children, and Brett was a special interest in the needs of chilren with disabilities. And she told the story of how Brett befriended a handicapped boy in his Little League playing days, was his roommate when others would not be, and who would become a lifelong friend. She stayed around for a long time, posed for numerous pictures, and signed autographs. I truly appreciated the boost that the Favre's involvement has meant to our program.

The news media was good to us once again. Almost every local TV station was there. I did interviews for two of them. The newspaper had front-page coverage, especially with a photo of Deanna Favre and Dick Resch throwing out the first pitch. But, I really liked the radio segment done by reporter, Danielle Spina. She interviewed a few kids and parents and did a clip with the voice from James Earl Jones from the movie *"Field of Dreams."* It aired on radio WTAQ here in Green Bay and on WTMJ in Milwaukee. I was astounded when my brother, John Liegeois, from the Milwaukee area called me that next morning and said that he heard it on the radio there in his car.

With the national anthem that day we started a new tradition. I had purchased flags of each Major League baseball team that we had teams for. Before each game, during the playing of the national anthem, we raise the U.S. flag and then underneath it the two flags of the two teams playing. The higher of the two team flags is the home team for the game.

My family all attended, including my mom, brothers John, Leo, David, and their families, and my sister, Dianne. My youngest brother, David Liegeois and his wife Lorna, hosted a cookout for all of us afterwards at his house in Suamico to recap the day's events and wind down. Along with my mom, I was honored that Lorna's mom and dad, Al and Karen Raether made the trip from Upper Michigan to be there on that special day too. With Dean Alford as the guest as well, we all sat around the table as Dean and I told our stories about the Miracle League to all.

We netted over one thousand dollars on that Dedication Saturday from the concession stand, which just demonstrates the impact that the Brett Favre donation enabled us to achieve. The concession stand that we were able to additionally build provides an immediate income source for our program. On typical game days now, we will net about one hundred and fifty dollars per two-game night.

View showing the completed shelter and unfinished playground in relationship to the baseball field.

Dedication Day – Deanna Favre, center, and Dick
Resch, right, throw out the first pitches.

The Ribbon Cutting

Deanna Favre, Paul Liegeois, and Dean Alford.

The Teams enter through the balloon archway.

The Leadership Green Bay Group with Deanna Favre.

The commemorative brick circle and brass plaque.

THE SECOND SEASON

That second season we had grown to one hundred and twenty players on ten teams, thanks to the help of a recruitment effort from the Leadership Green Bay team, the publicity that we were now getting on TV, newspaper and radio, and just word of mouth, parent to parent.

In only two years we have a new rubber surface to play on, and a shelter for our concession stand, with bathrooms and storage for our equipment. The scene repeats itself all season long. The first game is at 5:30 PM. Parents and children start arriving at about 5:00 PM. While some need help unloading their wheelchairs and walkers, others make their way to the concession stand where they must sign in, get their buddy assignment, and then wander over to the field in preparation for their game.

By 5:00 PM the smell of popcorn, hot dogs, and pizza is irresistible. I, of course, have my evening meal of a hot dog and soda. Parents who just got out of work find the concession stand for their dinner as well. The public address announcer is ready to play ball and has music playing as he makes the usual announcement to check in at the concession stand if you have just arrived.

The umpire is dressed for the part with an umpire's blue shirt that has a Miracle League arm patch, and an umpire's baseball hat with Miracle League emblem. Being that all children are required to have a parent or guardian present, the crowd begins to thicken in the stands, too. There are ten, then fifty, sometimes finally one hundred or more seated for the game. There is always a cheering crowd.

After the ceremonial national anthem, it's "Play Ball!"

Ages of the children are four years to nineteen years. But age, nor size, nor ability matter in the Miracle League. The tallest player is over six feet tall. The smallest is just barely taller than the batting tee. It doesn't matter.

The first batter up today is 18-year-old Zach Melvin. Zach is a large young man and can hit the ball hard, so the buddies on the field are extra protective of their players for this batter. Zach was all smiles that day as his favorite high school teacher was there to watch him play. I usually am seated in the dugout by the public address anouncer to watch the games. Before Zach's name was called to bat, he came over to me with his broad smile to point out his teacher for me. He so wanted me to meet her, which I did later, after the game, when he called to her to come and be introduced to me.

Zach squeezed a batting helmet onto his head. When his name was called he stepped to the plate. Zach likes to be pitched to versus hitting it off of a tee. The outfield fence is only one hundred and fifty feet from home plate. Zach can hit it that distance easily. This time he connects with the ball and sends a grounder to the left, all the way to the fence. Like all the players, Zach smiles broadly again, one hand on his head to hold his helmet on, as he runs to first base, proud of his accomplishment. Zach knows the rules and stops at first base. Otherwise it surely would have been a homerun that he hit.

The left fielder's buddy helps retrieve the ball. Giving it to the player, the buddy gives instructions to toss the ball in to second base. With a toss and some rolling momentum, he baseball finds its way back to the pitcher. The umpire calls "time out" for the next batter to get ready.

While the next batter is being announced to come to bat, a minor commotion takes place out in left field, where one of the athletes is having a tantrum for a moment and sits down on the job. Not wanting to play the field that day, but rather just be a batter, the buddy of that player calmly escorts her to the dugout for waiting her turn to bat again next inning.

I sat watching, as another player out there on second base, was keeping occupied between pitches by tossing a ball a few feet, back and forth, to his mom, who is his buddy today. Attention span is short for some of these children, so tossing a ball is okay as long as they are ready for the batter when the batter is ready to hit. The buddy is the watchdog for monitoring this. The umpire watches too, for safety reasons, and won't put the ball in play until there is attention. The boy stopped tossing the ball for a moment and in an instant spontaneously pounced on his mom giving her a big bear hug.

Megan Vincent, on her new team for this year, the Orioles, was out in right field as well. Mom was standing by as her buddy, pushing Megan's hair aside so she could see the batter. She was in her three-wheeler. This year, however, it is much easier for Megan's mom to navigate her across the new surface.

Smiling at my observations, I can't help but praise the parents for the special love and caring of these children. That feeling just surrounds you. There are no parents harassing the umpire for a bad call; there are no outs, no balls, and no strikes. There is no complaining about playing time; every batter bats each inning, and all players play the field. About the only parent complaints, if you want to call it that, is when a child's last name is mispronounced. The public address announcer is usually promptly corrected by a parent in that case.

The next batter gets a hit and Zach advances to second base. Again he knows the rules to only advance one base and ackwardly came thumping to a halt at second.

As the next batter reaches base, Zach heads for third. I'm sitting in the third base dugout, so Zach is now near me as the runner on third.

He shouts to me,"I'm going to score a run, Mr. Liegeois!"

I clapped for him and encouraged him on, "Way to go, Zach! Good job."

After Zach has scored a run, he looked over to the grandstands to see if his teacher was watching. "Safe" is the call at the plate by the umpire, with arms criss-crossing to signify a run had been scored. Zach also glanced at the scoreboad where a run had been added to the total for his team. Pleased by his performance he gives me the high five, his helmet nearly falling off from the impact of his high fiving. Then he removed his helmet and neatly returned it to the helmet rack mounted on the inside dugout fence.

"Did you see that hit?" he said

"Yes I did. And you scored a run," I answered.

The scoreboard records runs, but in the Miracle League the game always ends in a tie.

Every batter loves to hear his or her name called, so a good sound system is essential to the Miracle League. Our sound system is set up so that the amplifier is in the shelter, and we have to plug in the mixer at the field by our third base dugout to set the announcer up. I purchased an appropriate office cart to mount our mixer on to haul it out and set it up for games. We have microphones, both corded and wireless. We have a built-in CD player, i-pod inputs, and mixing for four different devices at a time. The two outdoor speakers mounted on a twenty-foot pole work out just beautifully. Just as a tidbit, because the Village of Allouez considers the facilities open to the public, so should, the sound system be available to the public. Now, I didn't want just anybody to use our cordless equipment, our CD player, and top-notch mixer, so we reasoned that we would buy a second mixer, just for Village checkout, if needed. No one has ever used it that I'm aware of. So, with a separate cart for baseball bats, helmets, catcher's equipment and balls, I need to pull only two loaded carts, the sound cart and the baseball equipment cart, from the storage room onto the field to set everything up for our games. The walks are all paved.

This year Teresa Anderson volunteered to take over the buddy scheduling, and had some great ideas to improve it. Bless her heart for all that she does for the program, coach, with a child on the team, and as Board member, too. Add to this the buddy coordination. This time I would direct all volunteer inquiries to her. I no longer had to keep a list or receive calls for the volunteer part. I did keep the player registration part and the scheduling of the umpires and public address announcers. For buddy scheduling we added that each team would have an assigned buddy coordinator and that each week it would be their responsibility to check if any players were going to be absent for the next game, and vice versa for the buddy. Teresa would be the central coordinator who would set up the original buddy assignment schedule, and be the person that the team coordinators call with week-to-week changes. Teresa came to every game, at which we set up a check-in table for buddies and players. Teresa always had the scheduled roster assignments. The system worked pretty well provided the team coordinator was conscientious enough about it to check with the player's parents week to week.

We had more teams, so more team sponsors were needed. The originals returned, and I had a waiting list for the new teams. Life was good.

We need a Web site, I thought. I contacted the Miracle League office to find out if they had anyone to recommend, since I saw several Miracle Leagues around the country had web sites. I sort of knew what we needed on the site from browsing other league sites. Diane Alford did give me a contact that had done their national site, she said, and others. But after no responses to my e-mail, and phone calls to his office and cell phone, I figured this guy was non-existent, and left me thinking the customer service from him would be poor. I asked Diane of there was anyone else. Stephanie Davis, who is in the Miracle League office also, came from South Carolina, where she was one of the founders of a Miracle League there and referred me to her cohort, Michael Blandford, who was involved in their Miracle League project. He was a computer guy by trade, and was interested in doing our web site as a trial, in hopes of getting more Miracle League business. So it is that Michael Blandford developed our web site, maintained it, and gave me my own on-line access to update certain text pages, like donor lists, parent information and such. Michael has been a joy to work with. He not only started our web site, but for going on three years now, has not charged us anything but the domain name maintenance fee. I've never met Mike in person, but got to know him through our correspondence. I even got to know his young boys a little, and sent them Packer gifts from the Packer Pro Shop, since they were interested in the Green Bay Packers. I even sent them each a Cheesehead when Mike said that on one of their school show-and-tell days that they had to wear a hat to tell about.

This year, Michael announced that he was giving up the idea of recruiting more business from Miracle Leagues, so we are in the process of transferring our Web site hosting to Camera Corner here in Green Bay. We will get a reduced rate, but now we will start to pay for the site hosting.

Our Web site is: www.greenbaymiracleleague.com.

I searched around on the Internet and found a beeping baseball for the visually impaired children. It costs about thirty-five dollars plus a charger of about eight dollars. The ball has a stick in it. When you pull the stick out, it beeps. The visually impaired child can hear the ball, for example, when you place it on the tee or can go to the ball if it is rolling. One such child, a favorite of mine, who is visually impaired, is Baylee Alger. Baylee is nine years old, and has been blind since two years old. He was one of my wife Mary Jo's special education students at the school where she works, so Baylee already knew me as Mrs. Liegeois' "dad." Baylee is very gifted. He plays piano and all of us were proud of him when he later won a national Braille speed-reading competition tournament. His story was featured on TV. Baylee always knows my voice, and I always reach my hand out to him when I'm present. He amazes me.

When he got his new team uniform, the team being the Arizona Diamondbacks, he put the hat on and felt the Diamondback snake emblem which was a raised logo emblazed on the cap, and said to me, "How come the snake has fins on its back?"

I thought, "You can feel that and know what it is?"

We needed a few new coaches and I should not go without mentioning Dr. Frank Mattia. Dr. Frank is someone special to me. Dr. Frank is a neonatal physician (pediatrician for special care babies). When Dr. Frank contacted me and said that he would like to help out as a coach, I thought, no way is he going to have the time. But he makes time for these kids. And many of them he has seen as babies. Between himself and his daughter, Kassie, along with Kassie's friend, Katie Phernetton, who served as his assistant coaches, they managed well together to be at all games. In addition, Dr. Frank helps out as an assistant coach for the Southwest High School Football Team. Frank was responsible, along with the Southwest High School Head Coach, in getting the team members to do community service together in helping to install our playground.

Team pictures were taken early in the season, at the second week of games. In the third week, I wasn't prepared emotionally for what would come next.

It was the Orioles vs the Cardinals. When sign-in was complete, there was no Megan Vincent that day. It was not like her mom not to be there.

The night before her scheduled weekly game, Megan, now ten years old, passed away in her sleep. I have this mental picture of her scooting around on her three-wheel walker, always happy, and really enjoying the Miracle League. But, with cerebral palsy she had trouble keeping her head upright, and they say, suffocated in her sleep. I was informed prior to the game by her coach. In the opening address and national anthem, which I always do myself over the public address system, I made the announcement and had a moment of silence in her honor. With my voice cracking it was difficult to speak. The Orioles coach, Steve Jossart, organized a pass-the-hat collection to be done at the next week's games, for planting a tree at the park in her memory. Over four hundred dollars was collected. Steve also hurriedly contacted the photographer of the team photos that Megan had been there for the prior week, and had a framed individual photo with team picture too, to give to Megan's mom.

I attended her wake. So did many, many of her fellow Miracle Leaguers. Her three-wheeler was there, decked out with her Miracle League team jersey over it, her team trophy that she had gotten the first year, her first-year team photo, the framed team photo that was just given to her mom, and a poster board full of memory photos from Megan playing in the Miracle League. I knew that Megan enjoyed playing baseball, but I hadn't realized *how* significant the Miracle League was to this little girl and her mom.

I called Diane Alford at the Miracle League office, told her about Megan, and how that affected me emotionally. The Miracle League office sent me a baseball glove and ball trophy with Megan Vincent's name engraved on it, and a special card with it, signed by all of the Atlanta Miracle League staff. The poem in the card is so touching I am copying it here for you to read:

Hi Mom, Baseball Is In Heaven

Hey mom, do you know they have baseball in heaven.
I pitched for the "Angels" on my first day.

71

Moses was a bit annoyed. I got caught "stealing." He said they don't do that here…

Hey mom, did you know they ski in heaven. We ride atop the tallest clouds.

Holding our wings in very close. We make a swooshing sound……You call it "wind" down there…

Hey mom, do you know that they have cable TV here. I get to watch all of the neat stuff I could ever want…

Hey mom, do you know they have dogs in heaven. I got one today. His name is Jake.

He follows me everywhere I go and likes to lick my face.

So, mom, I guess what I am trying to say is, that things really aren't so bad. I miss you and my family.

I do have some good news though…

At night when I fall asleep, God said I can talk to you in your dreams. So those times I show up and we laugh and play…

They are as real as they actually seem. Promise you'll talk back to me ok? (I can hear you when you pray) …

Hey mom, do you know they have baseball in heaven. Oh that's right, I said that before.

I hit a homer just a while ago. Abraham and Gabriel came in for a score….

A cameraman came close to get my picture. Just like they do for the pro's on TV.

I had the biggest smile you've ever seen. I put my face close to the lens.

It was huge and filled the screen. Do you know what I said? Of course you do…I looked in it and said.

"Hi mom, Baseball Is In Heaven"

Megan's mom, Connie Rissling, wanted to stay involved with the program and especially wanted to help raise money for a handicap accessible playground addition that I had talked about for the future. She especially wanted to see that we added the special full body swings with harness that Megan loved. Connie still helps out on the schedule for concession stand workers and went on the speaking circuit with me to raise money for that playground addition.

Megan's passing away was emotional enough in itself, but it affected others, too. When I passed the hat that day to collect the money for Megan's tree, most people dropped small change and dollar bills into the hat. One gentleman sitting up near the top of the bleachers all by himself, reached forward and put a twenty dollar bill in the collection hat. I asked if he wanted change. He said no. Later that same man came over to me and identified that he was with one of the Optimist Clubs that donated, but did not see it noted in our program booklet. We talked about the program and I was aware that their Club was planning on contributing one thousand dollars. I would check. Then as we talked more, him telling me what a great program we had, his voice choked, he developed tears in his eyes, and walked away from me.

He later came back and said, "Thanks for sharing a tear with me back there. I'm sorry, but I had a brother who had a disability. He would have been twenty years old now. He would have really enjoyed this."

Turns out that their Optimist Club, in fact, did not send that donation in as planned. He followed up and we received it later.

Much like the first season, we had a coaches' draft, and a parents' and volunteers' meeting. This time, however, the parent/volunteer meeting was the day that everyone could pick up their uniforms or buddy shirts. All meetings that we have are conveniently held at the Allouez Village Hall.

We had contributing sponsors, once again for the trophies, the volunteer shirts, and for Family Fun Day at the end of the season. For Family Fun Day, since we now had a concession stand for food, we served free hot dogs, free Pepsi, and free ice cream treats. Advance tickets were needed, but were given free to families of the players. Over five hundred people were served the free family food!

Because we had grown to ten teams we played two games each on Tuesdays and Thursdays at 5:30 PM and 7:00 PM and one game on Wednesday at 5:30 PM, so each team had one game per week. Opening day and closing day were on Saturday, and we had one other Saturday, which was a Grandparents Day. On Grandparents Day, all grandparents in attendance get to go out on the field with their grandchild to line up on the baselines for the national anthem. The grandparents also got a free hot dog and soda from the concession stand. Grandparents Day is something special and something that we continue to have.

One of my favorite kids to watch is Joey Counard. He's played all three years so far. One time a photographer was at the game Joey was in. The photographer just happened to be there to shoot footage for a national award that Dick Resch was getting for his charity giving, like what he gave to Miracle League. The photographer asked permission to go out on the field during play for some action video. I said sure. Joey was up to bat. I knew Joey's routine. I told the photographer to watch Joey, and be ready to get his picture when he comes around to home plate to score. Joey got on base, then to second, and to third. It was his time to score. The photographer laid right down on the ground, aiming his camera from home plate to third base at Joey, not knowing what to expect. As Joey approached home plate to score, sure enough, as he always did, he did his usual showboating, got down on all fours and did a hands-feet walk for the last few feet to home plate, with the usual encouraging cheers from the stands. The cameraman just laughed, but loved the picture.

I received an award that year from the Green Bay Chamber of Commerce when I was chosen as one of the year's *"Fifty People You Should Know"* and was featured, along with those fifty people in their monthly publication called the *Bay Business Journal,(BBJ)*. Little did I know it would be the first of many. We had to attend a photo session. There was a reception held for the *"Fifty People."* I was billed in the feature as **"The Miracle Man"** for starting the Miracle League. Quite an honor to be up there with the likes of my friends Tom Zalaski, TV-5, Bill Ward, Procter & Gamble, Phil Hauck, founder of The Executive Council, and many other deserving community people. I received another award that year from my Optimist Club as "Optimist of the Year."

In April 2007, I was contacted to accompany Ryan Popkey, WFRV TV-5, to an award ceremony in Madison, Wisconsin, where he was being given an award from the Governor's Wisconsin Council in Developmental Disabilities for media, for his *"Sports Extra"* feature that he did on the opening day of the Green Bay Miracle League in the first season of 2006. He would get the award for the media production. I would get an award as the subject of the feature. I met Ryan there that day, and drove down with my friend and high school classmate that I've probably mentioned already, Ryan's dad, Dan Popkey.

In June, shortly after our season was underway, I received a phone call from Angela Kelly, TV-11 Fox News. She is the early morning reporter for their *"Good Day Wisconsin"* feature during the morning news and wanted to do a live segment at the Miracle League Field about the league. I would be more than happy to! What did they need? She, of course wanted me to line up some kids to show playing, and some parents to interview, but asked me for some ideas for, say, four interesting things that they could feature on their show in four different 2-minute live clips. The news runs from 6 a.m. to 8 a.m. These would be about every fifteen minutes live. So, I responded with some thoughts. We could have the kids playing in the opening segment and interview me about what the program is all about. For the second time slot, we would interview parents, for the third, interview some buddies, and lastly, since Baylee Alger, the visually impaired boy and his mom were there, we could demonstrate the use of the beeping ball. So, that was the plan. It was Monday. Could I get it ready for Wednesday?

We had to recruit players, parents and buddies to be present at 5 a.m. to set up. It was not even light out yet at that time of day! I called and e-mailed the coaches, and, without a problem over thirty-five people showed up! It was great, especially the segment with Baylee hitting the beeping ball off of the tee and running the bases. You can view this video segment of Baylee on the *"Good Day Wisconsin"* by going to the link noted in the Appendix of this book.

Additionally that year, I received a phone call from Kevin Rompa, TV-2 WBAY, Green Bay, asking if I would be on his *"Noon Show"* to talk about the new Resch Miracle Field. I was happy to, of course. The show was the next day. He just said to be there by 11:45 AM at the studio. That's it, I thought? I've got to have some props or this interview could be really boring. So, I brought along the beeping ball, and a sample piece of the rubber surface, and my brochure, so I could prep Kevin with an explanation about the Miracle League, including photos of the field, before he asked me questions about it. I arrived early. In the studio waiting room I was greeted by Kevin right on time, 11:45 AM. I showed him the props and reviewed the brochure with him. He really appreciated the props, especially. As we went on the air, live, we were seated at a coffee table. I was really pleased with how it went, demonstrating the beeping ball, and showing the surface sample. You would be amazed at how many people said that they actually saw me that noon on TV.

We played eight weeks. On some days that year, it was very hot. Thank goodness for the shaded dugouts that we now had. Rain-outs don't get made up, but I don't recall more than two days that were rained out. Our second season came to a close on Saturday, August 4, 2007.

School starts for these kids in late August. They would have a lot to talk about from their experience during the summer in the Miracle League, and in many cases, maintain contact with their new friend, the "buddy" that they had. Codey May, for instance, fourteen years old and a buddy, became good friends with his assigned player, Joshua Gebhart. They go to the same high school and see each other now. They actually exchange gifts at Christmas time and have done so since Season One. Joshua's parents always request Codey as their preference for the buddy. There are many other buddy relationship stories that I could tell. It's great to see this happening.

Finally, that year, in one of my more proud moments, I received an e-mail from the mom of one of the athletes, Nicholas Traub, fourteen years old, saying that Nicholas had a school project to write about a real-life everyday hero, and he had chosen me! "You are My Giraffe Hero…thanking you for sticking your neck out to make the world a better place for others," it said.

Nicholas was an eighth-grader at Pulaski Community Middle School just outside of Green Bay. "Would it be all right if he asked you a few questions?" she asked.

I was flattered. Of course I would be happy to. He sent the questions by e-mail. The questions began with, "What motivated you to start up the Miracle League?" It ended with a question that asked for any other information that you could tell about yourself that perhaps we don't already know.

As he did not know beforehand, I responded to Nicholas with something about myself that most others probably did not know as well, and that is, that I too, have a handicap. I have Parkinson's disease.

Megan Vincent with her mom 2007.

Joey Counard (Photo by Donn Bramer)

THE OFF-SEASON

August is the month that I visit my neurologist, Dr. David Kaufman, for my annual exam for my Parkinson's disease. I have had it for about eight years now.

Parkinson's disease, or PD, is caused by a lack of the chemical in your brain that controls movement. It typically starts on one side of the body, but will eventually affect both sides. I have it on my right side; my right arm and my right leg. Typical of PD patients is tremor, and slow-to-get-going movement in that arm and leg. PD patients, therefore, will sometimes walk or shuffle, for instance, with no movement of the arm, or drag the leg. The right side is my dominant side, so, handwriting is non-existent. A side effect is swelling in my legs and ankles, and restlessness in the legs at night. Sleeping is a problem. But, thanks to drugs, most of that can be controlled. I take a drug common for PD. I take it regularly, at least four times a day. It takes about one hour for the drug to reach the brain. When it finally kicks in, this is called the "ON" cycle. Then it wears off. This is called the "OFF" cycle. For me, a dose usually lasts about two hours "ON." Trouble is, I can't get it to stay "ON" seamlessly. I will review this with Dr Kaufman on this month's visit. I have to take another drug at night for my legs, or I would never sleep.

I have become pretty proficient with the use of my left hand, for brushing teeth, etc. As you can imagine, simple tasks, like hygiene, bathing, putting your clothes on, during "OFF" times, when you don't have the use of your right hand, when it just won't work, can be difficult

Early on in my diagnosis, I read Michael J. Fox's book about his life with Parkinson's disease. It is every bit the way Fox describes it.

You usually notice a slight tremor in one pinky or something and it gets harder and harder to push that pencil or handwriting gets smaller and smaller. For me, I first noticed a slight tremor in my hand when I would hold a spoon for eating soup in the work cafeteria. I dismissed this, at first, as caffeine effect of coffee or something. But not to be. In Fox's book, he talks about being able to disguise his affliction. Before he would go on stage for filming, he would take his dose of the drug, and sometimes stayed in that dressing room for hours until the "ON" cycle took effect. The same for me, although it is no secret to anybody that wants to know about my having Parkinson's, I time the dose, so that I'm ready when the Miracle League games are ready to start and I have to go out there. My movement and writing is perfectly normal...for a while.

I am also a runner, have been for nearly twenty-five years now. Exercise is good for and recommended for PD patients. I run at least two miles, three times a week, either outside or early morning at the Downtown Green Bay YMCA. This is a routine that I've had for years, usually at 6:00 AM when I was working at WPS, now more like 7:00 AM in retirement. Anyway, I can take a dose of the med when I get up. I'll start running, with my right leg dragging and my right arm hanging. It's slow at first. Then, after about an hour, just like that, it kicks in! I can run like "Forrest Gump"...for a while. I call it my Forrest Grump moment. The arm swings, my gate is normal.... for a while. I've run in the last twenty consecutive Bellin Runs, a 10k run here in Green Bay, sponsored by the Bellin Hospital. I time the medication and it usually holds up for the entire race. My usual running friend, Jim Rennes, knows my limits and runs my pace. Hey, I can still finish the Bellin in an hour and fifteen minutes or so. For Jim, that's nearly a walker's pace, however. If I have any gas left on my dose at the finish line, I will even pour it on just to beat Jim.

On my visit, Dr. Kaufman says that I'm doing remarkably well on the medication. He tried another drug to prolong the "ON" time. I am fifty-eight years old. I've made the decision to take these drugs early in my symptoms, rather than wait till I'm older. However, the benefits are known to diminish over time. I have friends that I can relate to who also have Parkinson's disease, my fellow co-workers and retirees of WPS, Al Pearson and Ralph Baeten, and my former neighbor Dr. Jim Mattson. We see each other regularly.

I said earlier in this book that I would talk about my retirement later. I am a mechanical engineer by degree from UW-Madison, and a graduate of the summer Harvard University Business School Strategic Marketing Management Program. For a good share of my thirty-three wonderful years at Wisconsin Public Service, I was the Marketing Executive. In the later years, I was in a small group called Corporate Planning, that worked for the Holding Company, WPS Resources, (now Integrys Energy), on investigation and evaluation of potential business opportunities, mergers, and acquisitions. There were four of us. That group has since disbanded, with three of us having retired and the fourth leaving the company. Parkinson's affected my work, as I had trouble writing, especially when required to take notes. I couldn't keep up. I was tired from lack of sleep. My restless legs affected my attention in meetings. I also had a life-threatening close call.

I had already had PD back in 2002, when I had a kidney stone attack. For anyone who has ever experienced a kidney stone, you know the excruciating pain that comes on with an attack. I experienced that pain one night, rolling on the floor, curling up in a ball. I had no idea what it was, however, and struggled with it until morning. Mary Jo took me to the St. Mary's Hospital Emergency Room. They knew right away that it was a kidney stone, but X-rayed, gave me morphine, and sent me home. The morphine was instant relief for the pain. The stone will pass they said. Yes, the stone did pass. But it wouldn't be the stone that would be serious; it was an infection that followed that was life- threatening.

That night, I developed cold sweats, had trouble breathing. My breathing was rapid; I could not catch my breath. I tried to tough it out until morning again, but not this time. Mary Jo packed us up and immediately went back to the emergency room at St. Mary's. They tested my heart for possible heart attack. That wasn't it.

They did blood tests. They asked if there was anything that I was stressed over.

I said, "Of course, I'm stressed."

The hospital assistant assigned to watch me was there with Mary Jo and me. Now they wouldn't let me take medications that I usually take during that time, my PD medication either. The assistant said, "Look at you, you are shaking."

I said, "I know. I have Parkinson's disease."

I laid there for hours. Mary Jo repeatedly told them and was insistent that it had something to do with the kidney stone. Blood tests finally determined that, yes, in fact, it did have something to do with the stone. It was an e-coli infection and I was carted to Intensive Care. I spent two days there flushing the infection out of my system, while there was constant testing and monitoring of my vital organs. I received the Sacrament of the Sick from the Catholic Chaplain. Finally it came around. My breathing rate went down. I felt fine again. The doctor said, " You were on the fence there for a while."

So, yes, my health had something to do with my decision to retire. Although I didn't have to take it, I was given an opportunity to leave and retired. Without being retired, I doubt that I would have had the time or the opportunity to found the Miracle League.

Why am I telling you all of this?

"When life deals you lemons, make lemonade." I know my limitations and know that, at times it will be difficult for me. While I openly am willing to talk about my PD, at Miracle League the focus is on the children, who have challenges every day of their own. God willing, I am hopeful that I can be the Miracle League Executive Director forever and ever, and plan to do so. PD affects you physically, but the mind is sharp. I don't intend to let my physical limitations affect what I have to offer. I've learned from these children and from their parents. No, life isn't always fair. I've witnessed that my symptoms are minor by comparison to what some of these kids face.

For the Miracle League we have made provisions for the future.

We have set aside a set amount of the contributions to serve as an endowment fund for future generations, so that if rubber surface playground repairs are necessary, the funds are there. This amount is between seventy-five and one hundred thousand dollars. In addition, looking forward, I am thankful for people like Teresa Anderson, who have quite capably taken over one area of the administration, the volunteers. I will be looking for transferring some additional responsibilities to others over time.

I was really getting into my calling now. In the off season of the Miracle League, 2007, my thoughts turned to envisioning that the entire Optimist Park become a handicap-accessible, barrier-free destination for kids of all ages, regardless of disability or not. My attention, therefore, turned to expanding the playground.

Expansion Plans – A New Playground

Although I did not re-enlist the services of our original fundraising group, I communicated to them, that I, personally, would be seeking funds to add an addition to the existing playground.

By this time I had proceeded to submit an application for 501c3 tax-exempt status for our organization. In addition to our community fund at the Greater Green Bay Community Foundation that we were using for construction and operation, setting up 501c3 status for the entire program would make things a lot easier, especially in paying bills. Funds to and from the checking account would be recognized as charitable and tax exempt. With the help of my son, Beau, an attorney who recently graduated from law school, we were able to find the necessary IRS documents and instructions on-line, complete the necessary filing, and for the IRS fee of seven hundred and fifty dollars, we are now a recognized charitable, 501c3 entire organization.

For the playground, I mentioned earlier that Megan Vincent's mom, Connie Rissling, wanted to help raise money. So, for starters, Connie had a sister working at Schreiber Foods in Green Bay, who knew of Connie's desire to raise money for the Miracle League playground addition. The sister presented a case for our funds to the employee charitable program at Schreiber and was able to acquire a ten thousand dollar grant. That was our first donation. I really appreciated that start. A presentation of the check was made at one of our Board meetings.

Playground designs and proposals were sought, but from only two vendors, Burke Structures and Gerber Leisure Products. All vendors are good, I'm sure, and all offer some discount. Gerber happened to be referred by the Miracle League office. Burke had some of the existing playground equipment. The plan consists of two phases of construction addition, one for 2008 installation, and hopefully one in 2009, all with a rubber wheelchair accessible surface. Approval was necessary from the Village Board, which was received. Again, the Miracle League would fund the improvements, but the Village would own the equipment. No taxpayer money was involved, unless one considered that the parks crew, in their normal parks work, helped out with moving dirt and landscaping afterwards. The target was eighty-five thousand dollars of the design to be installed in 2008, with about sixty-five thousand dollars of it in 2009.

Connie joined me in speaking to groups. We talked mostly to service clubs that we could get ourselves invited to. I would do my presentation about how the Miracle League was founded, showing the Miracle League video. Connie would tell her story about how much Megan had enjoyed Miracle League and now she would like to help expand the playground in Megan's honor, especially to install the special swings that Megan liked. We received a 100% response in terms of some level of contribution from every group that we spoke to as a team. One hundred percent!

Then there was a contact by e-mail from an Allouez business, Green Bay Home Medical Equipment, who inquired about being a sponsor in some way of the Miracle League. I informed them of the playground expansion, and sent them a listing of things that could have individual sponsors if they chose one or two. The equipment that was available for sponsorship ranged in price from four hundred to eleven hundred dollars. A donor would get their name on that piece of playground equipment. Well, Bill Stelzer, the owner, responded that they would sponsor the whole list, forteen thousand dollars worth! So, we had another major donor. Connie and I visited with Mr. Stelzer and it was decided, that, instead, they would sponsor two larger pieces of equipment, a sway fun glider and an elevated wheelchair accessible sand table, for the same fourteen thousand dollars, leaving the smaller increments of equipment for other sponsors. In addition, Mr. Stelzer graciously is committed to a similar donation for playground additions in future years, so we have an advance donor for our 2009 phase, too.

In April of 2008, I was invited to attend the *Volunteer Center of Green Bay and Wisconsin Public Service Corporation-sponsored Annual Volunteer Awards Breakfast* for my work with the Miracle League. I was flattered to be invited much less find out that someone had nominated me in two different categories for an award. One hundred and fifty persons in all were nominated by someone. There were over seven hundred and fifty people at the event. Accompanying me at my table, I invited Teresa Anderson, Board members Ray Kopish and Brad Lange, and my sister Dianne Niemann. My friend, Tom Zalaski, TV-5 news anchor man was the MC, when my nomination category came up. My name was called as the winner of the Schneider National Foundation – Volunteer Leadership Award. With it came a five hundred dollar check for the Miracle League and a nice speech by a representative from Schneider. I was astounded and am thoroughly grateful for the recognition. Tom Zalaski told the little story afterwards about how we were acquainted as friends that see each other at the YMCA in the early morning. Our lockers are nearby each other and just the day before, we talked about how Tom was scheduled to be MC for this event, while I told him about my being nominated and planning on attending. He said that he had all that he could do to bite his tongue as he knew the winners and that I had won.

With funds already in the account and additional funds raised, we had eighty five thousand dollars to commit. We committed to the Gerber design, Phase 1. Different proposals were posted by Brad Lange, Parks Director, for the public, primarily neighbors, to comment on. All of this pricing assumed that we would install the addition with volunteers.

With the newspaper's help again, contacts with the volunteer center, and an e-mail to our entire list of past players families and volunteers, we recruited enough help, I thought, to proceed. On a weekend in May, so that the playground would be ready for the June 7th start of our baseball season, we scheduled a community build. Gerber representatives and our sales person, Mandi Wilke, did a fabulous job at construction supervision. They knew where every part was supposed to go and how to assemble it. We served hot dogs and sodas to the volunteers, did some pre-assembly and layout of parts on Friday, and scheduled the build for Saturday, starting at 6:00 AM. The media again was notified, and TV-11, did their *"Good Day Wisconsin"* live during our early setup. TV-5 did updates live throughout the day, too.

One hundred and eighty-five people showed up over those two days, including the entire Green Bay Southwest High School Football Team and their coach, former Green Bay Packer and Buffalo Bills Linebacker, Bryce Paup, and finished the installation. Dr. Frank Mattia, whom I've mentioned, serves as one of our coaches and is also a volunteer assistant for Southwest football. He was responsible for organizing the team to be there that day. The football team stayed the entire time until the last cement for footings was poured. The number of people was beyond my wildest dreams.

I am thankful also for the exceptional help that I received for this project from my retired friends and former co-workers at Wisconsin Public Service, Glen Schwalbach and Russ Kopidlanski. If I needed a tool, Glen had it. When I needed help with anything on short notice, Russ was there. Both of these guys were like construction managers. Thanks, guys.

As I was writing this passage of the book I received a phone call from Dominion Energy Co, the owners and operators of the Kewaunee Nuclear Plant nearby, informing me that they have approved a grant of twelve thousand five hundred dollars from my application, toward the Phase 2 playground addition in 2009. So it looks like the playground expansion will continue as planned.

All that remained for our 2008 schedule was to install the rubber surface to that playground to be ready before the June 7th opening day of our third year.

The playground volunteer crew that remained at the completion of the day's project. In all, over 185 volunteers participated in the installation on Saturday, May 31, 2008.

Our Third Year - A Gala Event for Opening Day

With a Web site now, all forms and schedules can be found online. In the first year of the program, I had to e-mail copies of these forms to everyone, the player registration forms and the buddy sign-up forms. Some don't have Internet service, requiring that copies still be made and mailed by U.S. Mail. But for the most part, the Web site is a real time saver for sign-up.

An information brochure was again printed and donated by Wisconsin Public Service Corp. Each year, the recruitment gets easier as the word gets around about the program.

My friend and former State Senator, Jerry Van Sistine, retired and in his eighties, helps out as an umpire. He happens to be on the Board for the Syble Hopp School, the local school for special needs children. So, now, not only are the parents there telling other parents, my friend Jerry personally brings the program literature to the school to see that it is distributed. Recall that it was originally difficult to get information into the schools, even Syble Hopp. Several of the new players'parents this year said that they got the brochure sent home with the child. Some new parents even told me that they got the brochure from their doctor. Recruiting buddies gets easier, too, as most schools have now heard of the program. The local high schools all have a requirement for volunteer work in the community for graduation. This is a good source for our buddies. The newspaper remains extremely helpful and are always looking for news in their community section.

So, for 2008, we grew to one hundred and fifty kids on twelve teams. Players come from as far away as sixty miles. Having the longest commute, I think, is 14-year-old Cody LaCombe, from Marinette, Wisconsin, about 60 miles, yet he did not miss a game.

I would say that we had about fifteen children that did not return, either because they moved away, are no longer age eligible, or simply that I could not contact them and don't know the reason. But we had at least forty new players on our new season roster of one hundred and fifty.

We needed two additional team sponsors, for which I, again, had a waiting list. I purchased two new major league team flags for our new teams for our flag-raising tradition. For the volunteer "Angels in the Outfield" T-shirts, the same sponsor returned, Resource One Realty, but this year I wanted to not run out of shirts for everybody. Last year's shirts could be worn, if they had one. The two new buddy shirt sponsors were Rebath of Northeast Wisconsin and NewiTech. To be able to purchase more shirts, there were three sponsors then, at five hundred dollars each, and their logos were printed on the backs.

The jerseys and hats were ordered plus player insurance, once again. The coaches' draft, and parent/volunteer meetings were held. A program booklet was again put together, with the team rosters, and an updated donor and sponsors list. My fellow Optimist Club members would be helping with the distribution of these during the opening day and throughout the season.

With twelve teams, I set up a schedule where only opening and closing days would be on Saturdays, and we would otherwise play two games a night on Tuesdays, Wednesdays, and Thursdays. Each team would play one game per week. This meant a sixty-six-game season played over nine weeks.

I've recruited a full slate of umpires who share the duties according to a schedule. There is Jerry Van Sistine, Bob Fry, Bob McCormick, George Murphy (a guy who helps out wherever he's needed), Russ Kopidlansky, Jim Anderson, and on occasion, my son, Beau, Tony Steffek, Kurt Carpenter, Bob Klaus, and Dan Vandenovond. All are volunteers.

For the public address announcing, in addition to Doug Phillips, of course, and my brother Leo Liegeois, we now have the voice and good humor of my friend and colleague from the Public Relations area at Wisconsin Public Service, Todd Steffen, Jim Anderson, and on occasion, my friend Bruce Vanden Plas has helped too. Former radio personality, Shaun Mulhern helps out in a pinch. I even had to take over the announcing one time. These, too, are all volunteers.

We tried something different for managing and staffing the concession stand this year. With such a large number of games, I thought it would be a challenge for one person every week. So a Weekly Manager Schedule was set up. The weekly manager would have a key, and be there early, say 4:00 PM for the 5:30 PM game, to set up everything and be there to shut down at the end of the day. Volunteers, who would sign up to just help, would be scheduled for days of the week, and come before 5:00 PM. One person would purchase the stock. That would be me. I would bring the cash box and take it home at the end of the day. The weekly managers alternated. No one had too many days. Parents with a child playing got to watch that child.

You will find that people will come forth in creative ways with talents that they have to help out. Thank you to many, many others like Julie Gregorich, for instance, Joseph Gregorich's mom, who made "baseball" themed aprons for all of the concession stand workers to wear. Seeing a need, she used her sewing skills to donate the aprons to the cause. They really added a nice touch to the atmosphere of baseball.

In keeping with my dream to make this a memorable "Disney World " experience for the kids, a gala opening ceremony for the season was once again planned. This time, I was contacted by the Green Bay Packers office, offering to arrange a player or two for appearances. I was thrilled and arranged with them for the players to be there, any players that they could recruit, at the opening day. Aaron Kampman, All-Pro Defensive End, volunteered and was going to attend, but he would be called away to his assist his father, whose home in Iowa was destroyed by a tornado. Players alternately attending would be Scott Wells, the starting Center for the Packers, Desmond Bishop, a Linebacker, and Johnny Quinn, a Wide Receiver. They were accompanied by Cathy Dworak, the Packers Community Relations Director. The players each had their Packer's jersey on with their number. It was awesome. Red-white-and-blue buntings decorated the fence and the "Home of the Miracle League" banner was tied up high on the backstop, once again.

I contacted all of the local TV stations again. TV-11, the Fox affiliate, even wanted to do their live, *"Good Day Wisconsin"* filming with us as we set everything up in preparation for the big day. The filming starts at 5:00 AM. With all that I had going on in things to set up, it would be a challenge to arrange some kids that they wanted to be there that early plus get some mascots and parents. But I guess that I'm getting the hang of accommodating things like that for the media and I wouldn't miss the opportunity for anything. So we were live on the air at 5:00 AM that morning with four different 3-minute segments between 5:00 AM and 7:00 AM. Our opening ceremony was at 9:00 AM. All of the other media was there too, the newspaper as well. I added links to all of the TV and newspaper coverage to our Web site under "News." However, if you click on the video links, there may be a time limit on how long that they archive them. Some of those older video reports for the Miracle League of Green Bay can be seen on-line on "YouTube." I didn't know that we would be that famous. TV-2 and TV-11 and TV-26 were there. The Green Bay Press Gazette covered our opening day also.

My sister-in-law, Nancy Steffel, again volunteered to arrange all of the mascot character appearances. The mascot from the local baseball minor league, the Bullfrogs, was added. The "Fly-Guy" was borrowed, once again, made possible by the Oneida Nation. I was the MC. My place on the field is always the pitcher's mound with a cordless microphone.

I started the Ceremony with the usual welcome, but then followed with a representative from the Volunteer Center of Green Bay, who wanted to re-present the award to me that I had been given at the Annual Volunteer Awards in April. They wanted to present it again in front of the Miracle League parents. Jules Bader, the current President of the Volunteer Center and grandfather of Noah Bader, for whom he is a buddy, read a tribute that made me proud of the award all over again. I brought the plaque with me so that he would have it to show. In addition, since the photo that they used in the plaque frame, was the picture of me and Ryan Blashka showing him throwing out that first pitch of the first game in the first season, I invited Ryan and his mom to come out on the field with me when the plaque was displayed. He was all smiles and got to meet all of the Packer players personally for photos.

This year, I wanted to add a special "Thank You" and recognition to all of the donors of over five hundred dollars a year, that have contributed each of our first three years. After all, these kind of donors are so very important. I especially wanted to recognize the Knights of Columbus – Abbot Pennings Council, for their on-going contributions and support. They have donated between five hundred dollars and one thousand dollars each year, and want badly to be a team sponsor, but they are next on my waiting list. Maybe next season, I thought. I am so thankful to them, regardless. There were eight of the repeat donors that I called upon to come out onto the field during my opening ceremony and receive a Miracle League pin from the Packer players who I had help me with this. These donors stayed out on the field for the national anthem, our Optimist Club members directing them where to stand on the baseline between second and third base, so that they could turn and face the flag which is outside of the left field fence next to our scoreboard.

Then, we had select children from the Green Bay Boy Choir sing the National Anthem. One of the moms, Lisa Hubbard, also one of our coaches, arranged for that. Her son, Jonny Hubbard, was in the Choir and was on the field with eight others to sing. I arranged for our sound system vendor, Northern Sound Contractors, a division of Henri's Music in Green Bay, to wire up two additional cordless microphones to our sound system and mic stands near first base, on the field, for their singing. They did this for me at no charge.

The players who were in the dugouts during the ceremony with their coaches and buddies, the public address announcer, and the umpire were all ready. With the short thank you ceremony, my award, the welcome, the intro of each Packer player and a few words from all of them, the players were called to come out and line up on their respective base line for the singing of the national anthem. Those children from the Boy Choir did a fabulous job. As was the tradition now for every game, when the U.S. flag is raised during the singing, below it are always the two flags of the teams playing that game, the higher flag being the home team. With the national anthem done, the home team that I announced takes the field, while the visitors return to the dugout to bat. This day, however, when all was ready, I would have the three Packers players throw out a first pitch. I purchased a few special Miracle League baseballs with the logo on them from the Miracle League office, for each Packer to keep after the pitch.

My routine to close the opening ceremony became…introduce the teams and their sponsor's name "for today's exciting matchup," then introduce and thank the public address announcer for the day's game, then introduce the umpire and proclaim "Umpire, are we ready to play ball?" To which the umpire yells into the microphone that I hand him, *"Play Ball!"* Music plays, announcer calls the name of the first batter up, game begins. Only, today we first have the three Packers still out on the field that each took a turn tossing a pitch to the umpire. Then we began the game.

Parents came early for the games, even if their team played later in the day, just to see the ceremony and the Packers. With the added teams, the concession stand that day netted one thousand three hundred dollars. That's pretty good, considering I want to keep the price of everything low enough and reasonable for a family to buy. We get a pretty good discount on natural-casing wieners that everyone raves about, from Olsen's Piggly Wiggly in Howard. And, they give us buns for reasonable cost, too. So, we need to make a small margin for the program and to cover all expenses, but I try to keep the cost of that hot dog to one dollar. Happy Joe's Pizza, Green Bay, delivers pizza-by-the-slice all individually boxed, for each game, in a thermal insulated metal box, kept warm by a lit Sterno can heater. We pay for what we sell. We sell a slice for two dollars. We will sell about twenty-four slices on a 2-game night. They take back any unsold slices. This works out really well. They have been most accommodating to us, and have good pizza. Please patronize them if you get a chance. The popcorn seed was donated, and on our special free food days, the Pepsi distributor either donates or steeply discounts what we plan to give away. The rest of the items we buy wholesale-- nachos, cheese, and candies. *No Gum!* We especially don't want chewed gum on the rubber field. So, all of these arrangements help keep our prices reasonable.

I spoke with Packer player Scott Wells a little. He was impressed by the program and said that he was unaware of it before that day. He told me that he had a brother that has a special needs child who would be moving to Appleton in the near future and would tell him about this opportunity. I sent him an information flyer. All of the Packer players stuck around for pictures and autographs. I thanked Cathy Dworak of the Packers immensely for thinking of us and participating. See their photos posted on the Green Bay Packers web site. The link to the site is noted in the Appendix of this book. Kathy said to contact her again next year.

The season was again, wonderful. I continue to take action photos at games and love to do so. But, now two different photographers who are involved in the program also have lots of action photos posted on their web sites. One who is a team sponsor, Donn Bramer Photography, whom I mentioned previously, and the other is Jeff Kralovetz, from Ambrosius Studios in Green Bay, whose wife is a coach and whose daughter is on the team. Donn Bramer's site link is repeated below and Ambrosius' link is added:

www.bramerphoto.smugmug.com

Direct link to Miracle League photos:
http://www.bramerphoto.smugmug.com/gallery/5633071_kZDK6#346192227_SRofE

www.ambrosiusinc.com

Direct Link To Miracle League Gallery:
http://ambrosiusinc.morephotos.com/mp_client/pictures.asp?action=viewphotos&size=thumbnails&thumbpagenum=1&eventid=47909&eventstatus=0&categories=no&keywords2=no&groupid=%20 0&bw=false&sep=false&ckw=false

We don't make up rain-outs. This year there were one or two, especially in the early season. I would make the rain call and usually, if it rained earlier in the day, the field would drain, and we would still play. Otherwise, I would call the coaches for cancellations. One day there was a downpour that cleared up by 4:00 PM. The field was perfectly drained and dry for our games at 5:30 PM. So, with the rubber surface, you can play on it, where normal grass would probably be too wet. The exception is if we had any lightning, that would be it. We would call the game. That happened once to us.

I think one of the classiest things that I witnessed all season, was on the part of the Little League coaches from the nearby Village of Luxemburg, Wisconsin, Coach Mark Jandrin and Coach Todd Jorgenson. The newspaper article read, "Baseball players trade practice for life lesson." One of our Miracle League athletes from Luxemburg, Carson Kinnard, loves baseball and is a regular in the stands at many different local games, including regularly watching his 8, 9, and 10-year-old peers at their Little League games. Despite being in a wheelchair, Carson plays weekly himself in the Miracle League of Green Bay.

Coach Jandrin worked with his friend Rob Kinnard, Carson's dad, to plan a surprise trip to one of Carson's games. Coach Jandrin and Coach Jorgenson, eleven players in their uniforms, and a handfull of parents took in the experience of a Miracle League game on July 9. Carson, a usually smiling child, was surprised and touched by the visit. He beamed from ear to ear as photos were taken with team members. I asked the coaches to do the honors of flag-raising that day. Those Little Leaguers in their Blue Jays uniforms stood at the fence, very well behaved, for Carson's entire game, and had a lot of fun learning the batter's names as they were announced over the public address system, cheering players on as they rounded bases, and slapping high fives as they crossed home plate.

Rob Kinnard said that the kids "took something very special out of that experience, learning a lot more from seeing these other kids experience the pure joy of baseball than from a 90-minute practice."

I continue to get speaking requests from service clubs to talk about the Miracle League and I love to do so. Now my friends Tom Dallman and Cheri Long have bought me a Panasonic video projector for these presentations. It really saves me time and I always know it will work. Otherwise, I needed to track down a projector from somebody, a lot of times from WPS, and make a special trip to try it out at the speaking facility to make sure it all works with my CD. I hate surprises, for example, to show up and find that your CD won't play on someone else's projector.

I was invited to visit Raymond Middle School, in Franksville, Wisconsin, a rural school near Milwaukee, by their physical education teacher to give a talk to seventh and eighth graders about the Miracle League. He wanted to not only demonstrate the activities available to children with disabilities, but to have them experience it as well. So we devised some activity stations, one to bat off of a tee blindfolded, to hit a ball while sitting in a wheelchair, one to field a ball blindfolded, and one to operate a wheelchair to "run" bases. I explained the Miracle League, showed the video, and then had the groups of kids rotate to try their hand at the activities. They all, of course, knew who Brett Favre was, and cheered when I noted that the Favres were a major sponsor. I repeated this for two classes. Those seventh and eighth graders had a ball. It was quite a drive for me to go there, but was a rewarding experience, nevertheless.

I think one of the most humorous requests that I received while at the field, was from an assistant coach, who shall remain nameless. Between innings of their game, when her team was scheduled to go out in the field, she had a bag full of coloring books and crayons, and asked me if it would be okay if she let the kids have coloring books in the outfield to keep them occupied. I must have looked at her quite strangely, but I said, no, I didn't think so. This is baseball. The buddies need to be on the alert for hit balls and the safety of the kids in the outfield. No coloring books.

As I mentioned before, prior to every game I would recruit someone in the crowd to do the honors of raising the flag during the national anthem. On one special occasion, my mom, Ann Liegeois, eighty two years old, who visits to watch the games often, driving from Marinette, Wisconsin, sixty miles away, was there that day with her visiting sisters from Florida, my aunts Theresa Szubartowski and Gen Zeglin, also in their eighties. Accompanying them was Aunt Theresa's special friend and my friend as well, Alwin Chaltry, from Menominee, Michigan. For those that don't know already,

Menominee, Michigan, in Michigan's Upper Peninsula, borders Marinette, Wisconsin, on the boundary waters of the Menominee River. I grew up in Marinette. I probably mentioned that already. Anyway, I asked Alwin to do the honors. He was thrilled. Alwin, eighty-nine years old, is a U. S. Marine Corp veteran who served his country in the Battle at Iwo Jima. I could listen to his stories about the War for hours. I introduced him to the parents and fans that day for the flag raising, and mentioned the fact that he was almost ninety years old, and a Marine Veteran of the Battle of Iwo Jima. Alwin was proud that day and for good reason. Many spectators, young and old, just casually stopped by him to either shake his hand or just say "thank you."

At one of our last games of the season, I noted that my friend, State Senator Rob Cowles, who happens to be a resident of Allouez, pulled up in the parking lot before the start of our 5:30 PM game that day. I was honored at his presence and thought that it was great for him to take the time out of his schedule to stop by. I planned on introducing him at my opening that day and did call him out to the pitcher's mound by me. I introduced him to the spectators and had him offer a few comments, then stay out there with the kids for the national anthem. Then I had him throw out the first pitch. It was great to have him. But that is not why he was there.

As I concluded my remarks, he said, "Wait one minute", and took the microphone from me. Jerry Van Sistine, whom I've mentioned previously, was the umpire that day, and was a former State Senator, too. Jerry came out to the pitcher's mound holding a plaque. Rob Cowles was there that day to present me with a "Wisconsin State Senate Citation" for my volunteer work for the Miracle League. As he read the complete citation, signed by the Senate, I was in awe that someone would think of me for such an honor. I will also cherish that award. It means a lot to me. I learned that both Jerry and Rob initiated the idea and pursued the award for me. Thank you, again, Rob and Jerry.

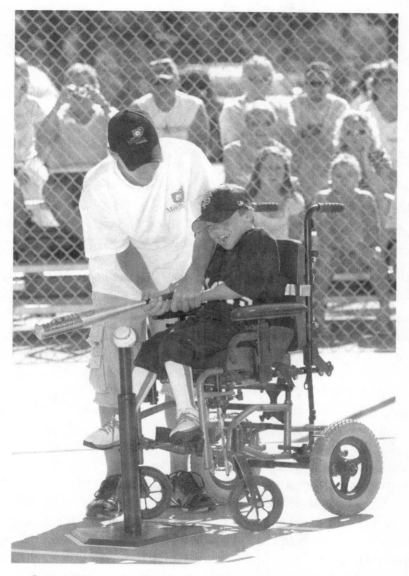

Carson Kinnard – On the day that his Little League Team
of friends showed up for Carson's Miracle League game.

(Photo by Donn Bramer)

THE GRANDE FINALE

I had a special idea for the closing ceremony this year. Since by our closing date, August 9th, 2008, the Beijing Olympics would be just underway, why not an Olympic theme? Besides, we had Olympic music.

So, with the usual planning that went with ordering the trophies, and ordering the food that we would serve at the Grande Finale for Family Fun Day, I got busy with some Olympic ideas as well. My good friend, Ray Kopish, had a battery-operated Olympic-type torch. It was a torch-shaped flash light sort of thing. A light shined up when you turned it on and a small fan in it blew upward on a piece of fluttering gold fabric. With the light and fan simulating a flowing flame, it looked like a real lit torch. This would be a perfect prop for what I had in mind. I borrowed it.

My idea was to have all of the kids present with their respective teams, coaches and buddies, all march in carrying their team flag. Leading them and carrying the torch would be any 19-year-olds, for which this would be their last eligible game, the graduating players. Then, I arranged for a scissors lift to hoist a photographer high up above the backstop to take a picture after all teams were on the field with their flags. The media was invited, too. After the picture, I would place the twelve team flags equally spaced and upright on the outfield fence for the day. I thought it would look awesome.

So, I built twelve flag poles out of PVC pipe, each seven feet long, and flag pole holders for mounting on the fence, which were just made from PVC pipe of the next size larger. I also constructed, out of lumber, a holder for standing all flags upright while they were being distributed to the respective teams in the staging area.

With the Olympic theme idea, I needed lots of additional help at the ceremony. My Optimist Club members would again be there to help. In addition, I had plenty of help, starting at 5:00 AM to attach the flag pole holders to the fence and set up the players' staging area.

The food was ready, and the concession stand staffed as needed. Tickets were required, once again for the family free food. We served nearly six hundred to feed this time. The good Olsen's Piggly Wiggly wieners and bakery fresh buns were a hit. They are so good on a summer day watching baseball. Then there were the free ice cream treats from Breyers Good Humor again and a Pepsi. Awesome! We did have sponsors for the food and the trophies again.

The ceremony went off as planned. I was the MC. For one last time, I would get to announce my usual greeting of,

"Welcome, once again, to Allouez Optimists Miracle League of Green Bay."

Optimist Club members directed the kids on where to march. They came onto the field from the left field entrance, down the third base line to home plate, to first base, all so the parents could see them, and then lined up on the infield. The "Elders," those carrying the torch for their final game, all had their names announced.

John Champ, 19 years old, from De Pere, Wisconsin, was the torch-bearer. He was the first player in the march to lead the others onto the field. As I stood there, at the pitcher's mound, microphone in hand, I could see the pride on John's face as he held that torch high. He proceeded to follow the direction of the Optimist Club members that pointed the way for the procession, proudly walking past all of the parents, siblings, and spectators, gathered up to the fence to watch. I could tell that John took his assignmet seriously. That made me feel rewarded inside that I had done something special that these kids appreciated in having a special ceremony like this.

The marchers were positioned at second base. The teams carried their flags in, at least those that could attend the early ceremony. If their game was later in the day, they might not have been there for the flag ceremony, but all teams had someone to represent them. The lift for the photographer was furnished to us and operated for us by Voss Electric, Tim Van den Heuvel. Thank you, Tim. After all teams were on the field, we took the photo. It is posted on Ambrosius Studio's web site. What an effect.

Then with the players lining up for the national anthem, the two team flags playing in the current game were hoisted as tradition on the flagpole. After the anthem, the other ten were placed on the fence in the holders. After each game we would alternate the next teams' flags for the next game.

It was a great Grande Finale.

Our field would win another award in 2007, this time for Brad Lange, Allouez Parks and Recreation Director, from the Wisconsin Parks Association. Thanks to the alert work of my friend, Ray Kopish, a Village Trustee, who noted the application for the award, the forms were filed for the award and recognition of Brad for the parks beautification and improvements made for the Miracle League Field. I helped Ray with the documentation and photos required. The Allouez Optimist Park was, in fact, selected and Brad received the award at the Wisconsin Parks Association convention in October.

People have helped in so many ways over these past years, I can't even mention them all. But another special person is my godchild, Kaitlyn Trader, 13 years old now, daughter of my good friends Jim and Cindy Trader. Kaitlyn, although not old enough to be a "buddy", came to several of our games with her mom. She even knows some of the athletes from her school and would cheer them on. Little did I know that Kaitlyn and her mom were capturing the moments with their camera, and as a surprise, presented me with a complete scrapbook, beautifully done to savor those memories from our three seasons to date. There are more pages and I hope that Kaitlyn adds to that book for me.

Following that season, in November, I got a phone call from an Alan Shipnuck, Senior Sports Writer from *Sports Illustrated* magazine, late one Friday evening. He was doing a story about Brett Favre, wanted to include a section in the article about Brett Favre's and Deanna Favre's charitable giving, and heard about their involvement with the large contribution to the Miracle League of Green Bay. Mr. Shipnuck said that he was on his way from Los Angeles to Green

Bay for the weekend's Packer home game and was going to interview Brett Favre on Monday. Would I be able to get some kids and their parents together for an interview also on either Monday or Tuesday evening, he asked. I was thrilled. To be in *Sports Illustrated*! Of course, I could get some kids and their parents together. He would confirm the exact time later when he got to Green Bay.

So, I contacted Teresa Anderson, once again, for doing some calling to parents, and I contacted another coach, Jan Phillips. I e-mailed some of the other coaches, but Alan said he needed only two or three families. The date and time would tentatively be either Monday or Tuesday at 5:30 PM. Alan confirmed the date to be Monday. I arranged that we meet at the Allouez Village Hall. We would then be nearby the field, which is on the same side of the street and just two blocks from the Village Hall, so I could show Alan the field.

Alan called by cell phone from his rented car. Seems that with the directions that I had given him, he had passed by the Village building and was a few blocks north. It was already dark outside. When he described where he was to me on the phone, stopped in front of a church, I said that he should look to the left side of the street. He was parked right in front of the Field. So, that's how he got to see the facilities, first hand. I drove there also with him later.

He arrived at the Village Hall at 5:30 PM. The Vanden Bergs with Jacob showed up, Carley Phillips and her parents were there, Teresa Anderson and daughter, Emily, and Kyla Willems and her parents. I showed Alan the Miracle League video so, as an introduction, he would know what the program was all about. We also showed him some pictures so he could see what the facilities looked like. The interview lasted about a half hour, talking with all of us as a group.

The story, it turned out, was for the December 10, 2007, *"Sportsman of the Year"* issue of *Sports Illustrated*, (*SI*), with Brett Favre on the cover. The Miracle League of Green Bay was written about in it, pages 49 and 56, from the interview that day. I was a little disappointed that I, personally, didn't get mentioned in the article. Hey, what man wouldn't like to see his name in *SI*? But there it was, the interviews with Jacob and his dad, Kyla and dad, and Carley's dad too.

As soon as the publication hit the newsstands, it was sold out in minutes here, locally. I could not get a copy. I called and e-mailed friends and relatives in other states and cities to see if they would try to get me copies. I was able to get a few copies that way but, shortly after the sellout, *SI* reprinted 50,000 copies, I am told, for the local market. I placed an order for copies from the Packers Pro Shop. All of that reprint production got sold out, too.

Sports Illustrated went on to produce other Tribute publications about Brett Favre's career (assuming that he was retiring from football). All of those publications, a *"Special Edition Tribute to Brett Favre"* magazine, and a *"Brett Favre – The Tribute"* hard cover and soft cover books, all contain a reprint of that same article about the Favre's charitable giving. I bought copies of those, too.

What a way to cap off the year.

THE FUTURE

September 9th, 2008, was the first Green Bay Packer regular season game this year. It was a Monday night game against the Minnesota Vikings. ESPN would be in Green Bay for *Monday Night Football*. ESPN established a "Chalk Talk" pre-game noon luncheon series which they hold in each of twelve host cities where they will be for Monday Night Football during the season. Green Bay was the first stop for 2008. The luncheon is by invitation only. The program in Green Bay featured the ESPN radio talk show hosts, and guest panel of former Packers players, Antonio Freeman, Dorsey Levens, Robert Brooks, and Minnesota Vikings former defensive back that defended against Freeman in his famous on-the-ground catch, Michael Griffith. The event in Green Bay was at Brett Favre's Steak House. As part of the event, ESPN and the NFL make a Community Service Award in each host community. I was informed by the Packer's office that they nominated me and that I would be receiving that Community Service Award.

I was invited to the luncheon with five other guests. My wife, Mary Jo, my sons, Nick and Beau, accompanied me, and I invited Teresa Anderson and her husband to join us. It was incredible. I received a plaque from ESPN. Mary Jo and I each got an ESPN duffle bag full of ESPN goodies, everyone in attendance got a canvas bag filled with stuff to take home, and the Packers gave me another bag filled with things from their Pro Shop, including an autographed football. In addition our program received a check for two thousand dollars from ESPN. Later that day, my family, the four of us, went to the game, tickets compliments again of ESPN.

Our fourth season in 2009 will be much like the past. I'm already thinking of some new twists for the Opening Day as I write this.

Continued funding will be needed. At some point I would anticipate we would have to pay some compensation for some of the present volunteered time. The Executive Director job is now nearly a fulltime commitment. Everything to-date has been volunteer labor. For 2009, we plan to add more equipment to the playground, with available funds. We'll continue to build the reserve endowment fund for future generations. I plan on continuing to be a fundraiser.

So far, we've been in the local newspaper eighteen times. I've counted the articles and saved every one. Four of those were front page, color photo features. The media has been good to us. I plan to continue to work on publicity.

For fundraising, I am thankful for people, like the Gosser's, Julie and Jay, whose son, Michael, played in the Miracle League for the first time this last year. They have been pleased with the Miracle League experience so much that they were instrumental in having the Miracle League be one of the charities to receive proceeds from the Annual Pink Flamingo Softball Tournament, a large event held in De Pere, Wisconsin. This year that meant over three thousand dollars. In addition, Julie Gosser, who owns and manages a De Pere restaurant called Caliente, donated proceeds from the sale of all "pink" drinks at their place during the weekend of that tournament. The pink drink promotion raised seven hundred and fifty dollars. They intend to do the same next year.

Then there was St. Brendan's Inn in Green Bay that sponsored a golf outing with Miracle League being the benefactor. This was the first year. I golfed in it. We had good weather and enjoyed the day. The event netted about one thousand five hundred dollars for our program. The manager, Berry Fitzgerald, said that he hopes to make this an annual event.

M & I Bank held a client charity golf outing as well and chose the Miracle League as the recipient of the funds raised. We received a check for one thousand four hundred dollars from that event. We hope that events like this continue.

Kevin Platkowski, owner of NEW *i* Tech, who is one of our Team sponsors and is a coach, is a racecar enthusiast. He and the

Anderson's, Teresa and Jim, recruited some additional parents to sell 50-50 raffle tickets at the Luxemburg, Wisconsin, racetrack. With the permission of the track, the proceeds from that raffle on that one night raised six hundred dollars. Thank you to all those who helped sell those tickets that night.

It is events like these and the wonderful support of many that I am hopeful will sustain the League for generations to come. Our funds held at the Greater Green Bay Community Foundation and in the Operating Checking Account, up until now, were basically held as non-interest bearing construction project funds. The Board has approved moving some of the funds now into interest-bearing CDs in consideration of maintaining that long-term perpetual thinking.

The appreciation expressed to me has been most heartwarming, knowing that your efforts are not going unnoticed. On December 11, 2008, my wife and I were invited to attend the University of Wisconsin - Green Bay men's basketball game to be recognized at halftime and on the jumbotron for the "Heroes Among Us" community service award sponsored by Prevea Health Care. I was nominated by the Volunteer Center of Green Bay for this recognition. It was an honor to be selected.

And, there was the 44th Annual Red Smith Sports Award Banquet in January, 2009, at Appleton, Wisconsin, where I was nominated by Associated Bank to receive a community service sporting award for the creation of the Miracle League program. This was also quite an honor as the Red Smth Banquet is one of the largest sports awards banquets in the Midwest, with all proceeds going to youth organizations throughout Northeastern Wisconsin. Over 1500 people attend this event. This year's speaker was Gene Keady, retired Purdue basketball coach, who will be introduced by Dick Bennett, former University of Wisconsin and UW – Green Bay basketball coach. Among the honorees were Doug Melvin, General Manager of the Milwaukee Brewers, and the University of Wisconsin Women's Hockey coach and a member of the 1980 gold medal Olympics "Miracle-on-Ice" hockey team, Mark Johnson. Quite a distinguished group. I enjoyed it immensely.

I have received inquiries from other communities right here in Wisconsin from parties interested in starting up a Miracle League.

There has been Madison, Oconomowoc, LaCrosse, Oshkosh, Wausau, Eau Claire, and closer to home, Appleton, Wisconsin. The parents, Lisa and Mark Robbins, of one of our players, Michael Robbins, and the grandparents, Gary and Sharon Lichtenberg, all of Appleton, enjoyed their first summer of Miracle League baseball in Green Bay so well that they are contemplating starting a league closer to their home in the Appleton area. I have met with them. We talked about what it takes to get it done. In fact the Lichtenbergs invited Mary Jo and me for dinner one evening at their home where they wanted to hear more about what's involved with starting up and running a Miracle League. The dinner was fabulous. We talked for hours. I probably repeated everything written here, so that they don't need to buy this book. I am happy to help them. They are wonderful people. I could feel their enthusiasm, much like how I felt on that initial inspiration, and know that we will be hearing about their Miracle League story in the future.

MISSION ACCOMPLISHED

I would receive one more award this past year. It was from the Rotary Club of Green Bay for Community Service. I again was flattered. I was invited to a luncheon to receive the award. I was asked to say a few words in acceptance. I didn't know exactly what to say this time. I said thank you, and that I am humbled and flattered to know someone would nominate me. However, as I had said on other occasions before, I told them, people don't do these kinds of things for the recognition, they do it for the kids. They do it for kids like Trystan Willems, who is wheelchair bound, nonverbal, and whose caregiver is his Grandmother, Wendy. Trystan goes to my church with his grandmother. When he sees me from across the way in that church on Sunday, I can see his eyes beam and a big smile when his eyes meet mine. His grandmother says I make him think of baseball. They do it for kids like Megan, whose mom said she enjoyed baseball in the Miracle League so much that they buried Megan with her jersey. And, they do it for kids like Tyler, (whom I've mentioned), that when he gets up to bat, raises that bat proudly, pointing it in the air, Babe Ruth style, but instead of pointing to the outfield homerun fence, turns to the bleachers behind him and points it to his mom and says, "This one's for you, mom." I said to those Rotarians, "This award's for you, kids! Thank you."

Dr. Kaufman says that my Parkinson's disease is very slow in progressing. I thank God for that. But, it is progressing. I thoroughly enjoy what I'm doing for these children, and the good Lord willing, I'll be healthy enough to continue for many, many years yet.

In October of 2008, Megan's mom, Connie Rissling, gave birth to a new, healthy, baby boy, Luke Rissling. I spoke to Connie on the phone, baby Luke testing his lungs, crying in the background.

"He'll be a good "buddy" for the Miracle League some day," she said.

Connie is still very much involved with the Miracle League, especially in further developments of the handicap playground that Megan loved to swing in. Connie continues to join me on presentations to groups to tell her story as well.

Resch Miracle Field at Allouez Optimist Park and the Favre Family Miracle Recreation Area are obviously special to me.

I have seen the "Miracles" of joy and happiness on the kids and parents faces over and over again. Although totally accidental that it happened that way, stemming from my visit with my friend Dean, I have found that niche of what to do with my life. Mission accomplished.

People ask me what my next project will be with the field. I answer, "Put a dome over it, and write a book."

Hana Platkowski at catcher. (Photo by Donn Bramer)

Paul Liegeois, second from right, receives the ESPN *Monday Night Football*, *"Fans Helping Fans"*, award for community service in creating the Miracle League of Green Bay at Brett Favre's Steakhouse. The Green Bay Packer's, Cathy Dworak, center, made the presentation.

The Liegeois Family – Nick, Beau, Paul and Mary Jo. Opening Day, 2007

Appendix

A. Cards, Letters, and Testimonials

"Thank you for all of the hard work you do to have this wonderful program. You really make a difference in our children's lives."

* * *

"Thanks for believing that all kids can play baseball. It is your vision that has brought us all great joy."

* * *

"Dear Sir, I would like to compliment you and your committee on the wonderful job that was done on the Miracle League Field."

* * *

"Dear Paul, Thank you for everything you have done for the Miracle league of Green Bay. It is very clear that you are doing the work you were meant to do. When we signed (our son) up for Miracle League, we had no idea how much it would mean to our son. He cried when a rain day threatened. (He) says that his career choices include becoming a pro baseball player some day! When the season ended, he wondered why Miracle League couldn't last as long as the professional season. We saw his hitting, pitching, and catching skills grow. When I think of his beginning gross motor assessments being in the first or second percentile, that's exciting! Miracles are happening right in front of our eyes! Thank you!"

* * *

"Dear Paul, We are so grateful for everything you do to make this league a dream come true for our son and our family. We admire the fact that you've taken on such a huge responsibility, especially in your retirement. You work harder now than you imagined you would in your "Golden Years." Thank you for another wonderful season. We often say prayers at bedtime to say thanks for special people in our lives..........you've been mentioned more than once. Thank you so much."

* * *

"Paul, We just wanted to thank you for getting the Miracle League started. (Our daughter) loved to go to each game (and didn't want to leave). Every night we had to play baseball at home. Her batting and throwing improved throughout the season at home. This is the first organized sport she has played in, as she is too young for Special Olympics and had a blast. We look forward to next year."

* * *

"Paul, Just wanted to let you know that my sister and brother-in-law have friends with a young woman (daughter) playing in the Miracle League. My sister saw her Thursday evening after the opening day game and she told her that it was the best day of her life!"

* * *

"As far as preference of nights to play the games, I'll make anything work! To see the smiles on my 2 kids' faces, I'd walk there if I had to.".........""You have made a dream come true for my two kids and that's all they talk about and show their pictures."

* * *

"…….Grandpa had tears in his eyes watching his grandson. He has two half brothers who are both sports fanatics and when his older brother saw him playing he said it was something he never imagined he'd get to share with his little brother. And for that dream to be made possible, I have to say THANK YOU PAUL, because you started it all"

*　　*　　*

"My son is really enjoying this (being a buddy), except on hot days! He even said after the first game, you know, mom, that was pretty neat this morning."

*　　*　　*

"Dear Paul, I just wanted to write you a short note to thank you for starting the Miracle League in Green Bay. Our first game is still one day away and it is all that (our daughter) talks about. She looked at her shirt this morning and turned to me and said, "Tomorrow I get to wear my uniform!" She is so excited that she gets to play baseball like her brother. It means so much to her and to us as a family. When she was diagnosed with a brain tumor we just wanted her to live. When we knew that she would survive but with many disabilities, we just wanted her to be happy. You have made her happy! Thank you so much. We look forward to Thursday's game."

*　　*　　*

B. WEB SITES

Miracle League of Green Bay:
For: Green Bay League information, registration, photos, parent
news, news links, to donate, contact us

www.greenbaymiracleleague.com

National Miracle League Association:
For: National Association information, merchandise purchase, to
start a league, contact info

www.miracleleague.com

Donn Bramer Photography:
For: Photo gallery of Green Bay Miracle League photos

www.bramerphoto.smugmug.com

Ambrosius Studios:
For: Photo gallery of Green Bay Miracle League photos

www.ambrosiusinc.com

The Miracle League of Green Bay – WFRV TV Documentary
For: See video documentary of the construction of the Green Bay
Miracle League Field

http://www.youtube.com/watch?v=Dlclv1Armb8&feature=related

"Good Day Wisconsin"- Featuring Miracle League of Green Bay - WLUK Fox 11 TV, Green Bay

For: Link to Video Segment from Feature with Baylee Alger

http://www.myfoxnewisconsin.com/myfox/pages/InsideFox/Detail
?contentId=3542749&version=3&locale=EN-US&layoutCode=VSTY&pageId=5.2.1

"Players Attend Miracle League's Opening Day"
Green Bay Packers Web site at www.packers.com

For: Link to Photo Gallery of Green Bay Packers Players at Opening Day 2008

http://www.packers.com/multimedia/photo_galleries/2008_
nongame/2008-06-07/

C.   DIRECTORY OF NAMES FOUND IN THIS BOOK

Name

Alford, Chandler
Alford, Dan
Alford, Dean
Alford, Diane
Alford, Jacque
Alford, Terre
Alger, Baylee
Anderson, Jim
Anderson, Emily
Anderson, Teresa
Audit, Mike
Bader, Jules
Bader, Noah
Baeten, Ralph
Baeten, Tina
Bagwell, Eddie
Barton, Larry
Bennett, Dick
Bishop, Desmond
Bix, Tyler
Blandford, Michael
Blaney, Patrick
Blashka, Connie
Blashka, Ryan
Borths, Scott
Bramer, Donn
Brittain, Jeanette
Brooks, Robert
Carpenter, Kurt
Chaltry, Alwin
Champ, John
Chernick, Rick
Cloud Family
Condon, Cort

Counard, Joey
Cowles, Rob
Dahlin, Amy
Dahlin, Bernie
Dallman, Tom
Daniels, Mike
Deford, Frank
Drew, Austin
Drew, Theresa
Dworak, Cathy
Eggars, Gene
Favre, Brett
Favre, Deanna
Fitzgerald, Berry
Fox, Michael J.
Freeman, Antonio
Frohna, Michael
Fry, Bob
Gailey, Chan
Gard, John
Gard, Kate
Gebhardt, Joshua
Gerczak, Ed
Gerczak, Mary
Giddens, Don
Giddens, Rebecca Bennett
Goetz, Jim
Goldman, Stu
Gosser, Jay
Gosser, Julie
Gregorich, Joseph
Gregorich, Julie
Griffith, Robert
Gulling, Dan
Gumbel, Bryant
Hagerty, Mike
Hauck, Phil
Hickey, John
Hoffman, Barb
Hoffman, Fred
Howald, Tim

Hubbard, Jonny
Hubbard, Lisa
Jandrin, Mark
Jartz, Bill
Johnson, Mark
Jones, Dave
Jones, James Earl
Jorgensen, Tim
Jorgensen, Todd
Jossart, Steve
Kampman, Aaron
Kaufman, David
Kawala, Lisa
Keady, Gene
Kelly, Angela
Kemper, Linda
Kinnard, Carson
Kinnard, Rob
Klaus, Bob
Kolarik, Joni
Kopidlansky, Russ
Kopish, Ray
Kopitzke, Casey
Kralovetz, Jeff
Kress, John
LaCombe, Cody
Lange, Brad
Lanser, Nick
Lemmens, Michele
Levens, Dorsey
Lichtenberg, Gary
Lichtenberg, Sharon
Liegeois, John
Liegeois, Ann
Liegeois, Beau
Liegeois, Bill
Liegeois, David
Liegeois, Leo
Liegeois, Lorna
Liegeois, Mary Jo
Liegeois, Nick

Liegeois, Paul
Long, Cheri
Long, Don
Mattia, Dr. Frank
Mattia, Kassie
Mattson, Dr. ,Jim
May, Codey
McClain, Ray
McCormick, Bob
Melvin, Zach
Meng Family
Monahan, Tom
Mossakoski, Laura
Mottl, Bob
Mulhern, Shaun
Murphy, George
Murphy, Pat
Nagarajan, Mythili
Naumann, Alan
Niemann, Dianne
Olson, Tom
O'Neal, Pat
Oswald, Randy
Paup, Bryce
Pearson, Al
Phernetton, Katie
Phillips, Carley
Phillips, Doug
Phillips, Jan
Pietrek, Joe
Pietrek, Aimee
Platkowski, Hana
Platkowski, Kevin
Popkey, Aaron
Popkey, Dan
Popkey, Ryan
Quinn, Johnny
Raether, Al
Raether, Karen
Raj, Robin
Ratchman, Michelle

Reinsch, Lee
Rennes, Jim
Resch, Dick
Rissling, Connie
Rissling, Luke
Ritchay, Jim
Robbins, Lisa
Robbins, Mark
Rogaczewski, Gary
Rompa, Kevin
Schmidt, Beth
Schmidt, Dr. Frederick
Schmidt, Laura
Schultz, Fred
Schultz, Paula
Schwalbach, Glen
Seidl, Steve
Shipnuck, Alan
Smith, Jacqueline
Smith, Red
Sperry, Wanda
Spina, Danielle
Steffek, Tony
Steffel, Nancy
Steffel, Sherry
Steffen, Todd
Stein, Lori
Stelzer, Bill
Strmiska, Ken
Sweasy, Bill
Szubartowski, Theresa
Tacshner, Jack
Thomas, Chuck
Tonelli, Rich
Trader, Jim
Trader, Cindy
Trader, Kaitlyn
Traub, Nicholas
Van Dyke, Neil
Van Laanen, Paul
Van Sistine, Jerry

Vanden Berg, Jacob
Vanden Heuvel, Tim
Vanden Plas, Bruce
Vandenovond, Dan
Vincent, Megan
Ward, Bill
Wells, Scott
Wickman, Bob
Willems, Kyla
Willems, Trystan
Willems, Wendy
Williams, Teresa
Zalaski, Tom
Zeglin, Gen
Ziegelbauer, Gary
Zubick, Bishop

D.   TO DONATE

For more information, to Volunteer, to Sponsor a child, or to donate:

Visit www.greenbaymiracleleague.com

Contact or send contributions to:

Miracle League of Green Bay
Paul Liegeois, Founder/Executive Director
2445 Shady Oak Drive
Green Bay, WI 54304

e-mail:

LiegeoisPaul@aol.com